BRECON BEACONS
>> TRAIL RUNNING

20 OFF-ROAD ROUTES FOR
TRAIL & FELL RUNNERS

Vertebrate Publishing, Sheffield
www.**v-publishing**.co.uk

BRECON BEACONS
» TRAIL RUNNING
20 OFF-ROAD ROUTES FOR TRAIL & FELL RUNNERS

Lily Dyu & John Price

BRECON BEACONS
>> TRAIL RUNNING
20 OFF-ROAD ROUTES FOR TRAIL & FELL RUNNERS

 First published in 2018 by Vertebrate Publishing.

Vertebrate Publishing, Crescent House, 228 Psalter Lane, Sheffield S11 8UT, United Kingdom.
www.v-publishing.co.uk

A CIP catalogue record for this book is available from the British Library.

ISBN 978-1-911342-27-4

Front cover: Tracy Purnell and Jen Scotney above Llangors Lake (run 5).
Back cover: Jon Drever climbing above Llyn y Fan Fach in the Mynydd Du range (run 16).
Photography by John Coefield unless otherwise credited.

 All maps reproduced by permission of Ordnance Survey on behalf of The Controller of Her Majesty's Stationery Office.
© Crown Copyright. 100025218.

Design and production by Vertebrate Publishing – www.v-publishing.co.uk

Printed and bound in Europe by Pulsio.
Vertebrate Publishing is committed to printing on paper from sustainable sources.

MIX
Paper from responsible sources
FSC® C128169
www.fsc.org

≫ CONTENTS

JOHN PRICE RUNNING UP AND ROUND TOWARDS TABLE MOUNTAIN (RUN 3).

>> INTRODUCTION

John, a keen – but very moderate – fell runner, has lived near the Brecon Beacons most of his life after growing up in a Welsh farming family. Always happy to throw himself down a trackless mountainside, this may explain his adulation of shepherd and fell legend, Joss Naylor. Lily 'comes from off' – as they say about newcomers – and generally prefers sticking to footpaths. Before moving here, her only experience of the area was climbing Pen y Fan, whose summit view of mountains rising and falling like a petrified wave still takes her breath away after she has lived here for ten years.

We became friends through our running club and have shared many days out on local hills and further afield. For both of us writing this book has been a joy – revisiting favourite trails and discovering new places, and in all seasons.

There are in fact four separate mountain ranges within the Brecon Beacons National Park. The most easterly is the Black Mountains, where long, interlocking ridges and deep river valleys create a sense of isolation. The Brecon Beacons themselves form only the central range, despite giving their name to the whole region. Here a steep escarpment rises above the Usk Valley to form a collection of smooth, rounded summits – the highest in the area. Further to the west lies Fforest Fawr, the 'Great Forest of Brecknock' – once a royal hunting ground and today an area of austere, lonely moorland. The most westerly range is the Black Mountain, the wildest and most remote part of the park, home to the brooding peaks of the Carmarthen Fans – Picws Du and Fan Brycheiniog. >>

There are also smaller regions with distinct characteristics, the most popular being the 'Waterfall Country' around Ystradfellte, while Mynydd Llangatwg is an expanse of limestone upland, riddled with shake holes, rocky outcrops, cliffs and cave systems. Industrial relics dominate the Blorenge mountain to the south-east, a UNESCO World Heritage Site. To the north of Hay-on-Wye are the Begwns, a National-Trust-owned range of hills, which although relatively low in height, nevertheless command stunning 360-degree views. Contouring through the southern reaches of the park are the tranquil waters of the Monmouthshire and Brecon Canal, possibly the most scenic man-made waterway in Britain.

The area has a vibrant fell running scene and is home to several ultramarathons, including the South Wales 100, an epic circuit of the mountains starting from Cardiff. Perhaps less well known, compared to its sister rounds like the Bob Graham, is the Brecon Beacons Traverse – a 72-mile, 24-hour fell running challenge across the entire range, from Llandeilo in the west to Llanthony in the east.

Through our selection of easy-to-challenging routes in this book, we wanted to share the best of the running and the varied landscapes in the Brecon Beacons, through visiting popular spots but on quieter approaches, and by shining a light on those equally deserving but less well-known places. Even if you have run here before, we hope this book takes you on to trails that you have yet to discover.

Happy running!
John Price & Lily Dyu

FEET FIRST.
HEAD WILL FOLLOW.
GET A GRIP

X-TALON 230 / INOV8

INOV-8.COM

ACKNOWLEDGEMENTS

Lily: My thanks to John, friend and co-author, for showing me so many new and special places to run; to all our Hay Hotfooters friends who have provided wonderful company and much laughter during days out in the hills; and most of all, thank you to Chris who brought me to these beautiful mountains.

John: My thanks to Lily for inviting me to become involved in this book and to my various running friends – particularly those who have saved me from potential disasters while on the hills on more than one occasion (you know who you are!). Thanks also to my family (Sally, Evie and Jess) who have not seen as much of me as they were entitled to expect over the last year or so while the routes in this book were being explored.

Vertebrate: Thanks to our dashing, willing and able photo models, Tracy Purnell, Jen Scotney, Jon Drever, Hannah Phillips and Jon Barton, and to Tracy Purnell, Alan Nicholls and John Price for their additional photography.

ABOUT THE ROUTES

The routes range in difficulty from relatively easy, undulating runs on reservoir paths or common land that will take less than an hour, to challenging fell runs and longer mountain routes. They have been ordered in terms of increasing length, but total ascent and terrain should also be taken into account too since these have a huge impact on the difficulty of the run. If you are new to trail running then start with some lower-level routes to gauge your level. Fan Frynych (page 19) could be a good first test of your hill-running fitness and confidence.

We have done our best to advise how long a route may take, however this is subjective and depends on the runner, the state of the trails, the weather, how often you stop to take in the views (or to rest) and, in some cases, your ability to navigate using a map and compass.

In addition to the total time, we've used **Mountain Goats** and **Navigation** ratings. **Mountain Goats** is on a scale of 🐐 (easy), 🐐 🐐 (medium) and 🐐 🐐 🐐 (hard), and **Navigation** is rated on a scale from **1** (easy) to **5** (hard).

For example:

A route graded **Mountain Goats** 🐐 and **Navigation 1** will generally be on good paths and tracks and should be easy to navigate in most weather conditions.

A route graded **Mountain Goats** 🐐🐐 and **Navigation 1** will be on terrain that is more technical. This may mean it is rocky, loose or muddy or that there is a lot of ascent and descent (or both), but there are plenty of waymarkers to look out for and the paths are still easy to recognise and follow.

A route graded **Mountain Goats** 🐐🐐🐐 and **Navigation 5** indicates that the terrain is very difficult (possibly covering open fell with no paths or tracks, very steep ground, and on loose, slippery and muddy terrain). Additionally, the route may also be more committing, being further from roads or without mobile phone reception. With regards to navigation, there are likely to be sections of the route which are without waymarkers and obvious features, making the ability to use a map and compass essential. Errors in navigation may be costly, leaving you hours from your start point.

Inevitably, each route will have certain sections which could be classified differently to the overall grade we have given for the route; thus a route graded **Mountain Goats** 🐐 and **Navigation 1** could well have sections which are more difficult and technical than these gradings suggest. In providing these classifications, we have tried to assess each route on an overall basis.

Likewise, the navigation ratings are very weather dependent: a Navigation **4** could be straightforward on a bright sunny day where you can easily see where you are and where you are going. However, in foul weather and with the mist down, even a Navigation **1** could provide a route-finding challenge.

MAPS
All the routes are carefully described and plotted on Ordnance Survey 1:25,000 mapping, but it is strongly recommended that you carry the relevant full map and a compass. **Explorers OL12** and **OL13** (1:25,000), and **Landrangers 148**, **159**, **160** and **161** (1:50,000) cover all the runs in this guide and are essential even if you are familiar with the area – you may need to cut short a run or take an alternative route. And of course, a map is no use without the navigational skills to use it.

DESCRIPTIONS, ESTIMATED TIMES, DISTANCES & ASCENT
While every effort has been made to ensure accuracy within the maps and descriptions in this guide, we are unable to guarantee that every single detail is correct (and things do occasionally change). Please exercise caution if a direction appears at odds with the route on the ground. If in doubt, a comparison between the directions, map and a bit of common sense should ensure you are on the right track.

Distances are in kilometres and height gain is in metres. Both were measured using GPS devices on the runs, but we cannot promise that they are 100 per cent accurate, so please treat stated distances as a guideline only.

Our estimated times are generally within a range and these are a combination of optimism, generosity, challenge and fiction; just allow plenty of time and try to run an even pace. Clearly the time taken to complete a route will be less if you are a fit, fast runner, oblivious to the views and can find your way around with only scant regard for the route descriptions and map. Those (like the authors) who are less speedy and who take reassurance from regularly checking where they are, and who stop to take the odd photograph or for a rest, will take longer.

Ordnance Survey maps are the most commonly used, easy to read and many people are happy using them. If you are not familiar with OS maps and are unsure of what the symbols mean, you can download a free OS 1:25,000 map legend from **www.ordnancesurvey.co.uk**

Here are a few of the symbols and abbreviations we use on the maps and in our directions:

 ROUTE STARTING POINT   **2** ROUTE MARKER

 OPTIONAL ROUTE   52 ADDITIONAL GRID LINE NUMBERS TO AID NAVIGATION

Intake fences and walls: For those unfamiliar with the term, an 'intake' fence or wall is a fence or wall that separates the open hillside from enclosed pastures.

TERRAIN

We've done our best to give accurate descriptions of the land, waymarkers and surroundings. However, it's important to remember that even relatively permanent features can change. Maps can go out of date, footpaths can be rerouted, woodland can be felled, rivers can swell and signposts can be moved or disappear. The weather can dramatically alter the state of the route, in particular those on open fells and less-distinct paths (and, of course, the weather in the mountains can change quickly). Paths may become even less obvious and too muddy to run on easily. On several of these routes in the summer months, especially in the Black Mountains, there may be bracken growing tall and thick around the paths, which can make navigation more difficult.

While there are rocky areas, running in the Brecon Beacons National Park is not as technical as in some other areas (such as North Wales or the Lake District). However, you will get wet and muddy feet – there are bogs aplenty!

TRANSPORT

The Brecon Beacons National Park is a sparsely populated, remote area and unfortunately has poor public transport links. Where a route is accessible by bus this information is included in the information box, otherwise you will require a car or bike.

RECOMMENDED EQUIPMENT

Recommended kit varies depending on the time of year and the difficulty and nature of the route. While many runners like the freedom of a 'fast and light' approach, longer and more remote runs are best undertaken with a little more kit.

» **Bag**: there are plenty of lightweight rucksacks and bumbags on the market. Find one that's comfy and doesn't move around when you're running on rough ground.
» **Waterproofs/windproofs**: jacket and trousers. We'd strongly recommend fully waterproof with taped seams – this is Wales after all!
» **Hat and gloves**: keep your extremities warm and the rest will follow. It's no fun fumbling with shoelaces with frozen fingers.
» **Map and compass**: and know how to use them! The relevant maps are listed on page XI.
» **Whistle**: six short blasts in quick succession means 'help!'
» **Space blanket and small first aid kit**: weigh nothing, take up hardly any space and could save your life.
» **Food and water**: enough for your expected duration of the run and some emergency rations (and maybe even a picnic for a longer day in the hills!).
» **Head torch**: if you're heading out late, a head torch should be high on your list of essentials.

FOOTWEAR

We recommend at least 'trail' shoes for all these routes, with fell shoes being desirable on the harder routes. Trail shoes offer more grip and greater stability than road shoes, while the deep lugs on the soles of fell shoes will come in handy on boggy or wet ground.

CLOTHING

Dress appropriately for the season and we recommend you **always carry full waterproofs** for any longer and/or higher runs, since the weather can change quickly. Shorts and a vest may work well on hot summer days, but thermals, windproofs and gloves are better on winter runs. Please note that exposure on higher ground is a very real risk for the tired, lost or slow-moving runner – better to carry a small bag with full waterproofs and gloves/hat, than to get into trouble on the top of Pen y Fan and have to call out mountain rescue.

FUEL & HYDRATION

Hot days can be deadly for the trail runner. We don't recommend drinking from any streams in the Brecon Beacons (this is sheep country after all!), so carry sufficient water (either in bottles or a hydration pack) for your run. Likewise, a banana or two and an 'emergency' gel can come in handy, especially on long days out.

SAFETY

Ideally, run in company. Always tell someone where you are going and carry a phone – but note that finding good reception is difficult in many parts of the Brecon Beacons. Should you find yourself out of reception, be grateful to be temporarily free of the phone's tyranny.

MOUNTAIN RESCUE

In case of an accident or similar requiring mountain rescue assistance, dial **999** and ask for **POLICE – MOUNTAIN RESCUE**. Be prepared to give a six-figure grid reference of your position.

MOUNTAIN RESCUE BY SMS TEXT

Another option in the UK is contacting the emergency services by SMS text – useful if you have a low battery or intermittent signal. You need to register first – text 'register' to **999** and then follow the instructions in the reply. **www.emergencysms.org.uk**

DOGS

While some of our routes have gates and stiles, most of them would be great for dogs (at least for those dogs fit enough and capable of running the required distance on open hillsides). However, the Brecon Beacons has considerable livestock and wildlife, so keep your dogs under close control and do what all respectable and sensible dog-owners should do.

THE COUNTRYSIDE CODE

RESPECT OTHER PEOPLE

Please respect the local community and other people using the outdoors. Remember your actions can affect people's lives and livelihoods.

Consider the local community and other people enjoying the outdoors

» Respect the needs of local people and visitors alike – for example, don't block gateways, driveways or other paths with your vehicle.

» When riding a bike or driving a vehicle, slow down or stop for horses, walkers and farm animals and give them plenty of room. By law, cyclists must give way to walkers and horse riders on bridleways.

» Co-operate with people at work in the countryside. For example, keep out of the way when farm animals are being gathered or moved and follow directions from the farmer.

» Busy traffic on small country roads can be unpleasant and dangerous to local people, visitors and wildlife – so slow down and, where possible, leave your vehicle at home, consider sharing lifts and use alternatives such as public transport or cycling. For public transport information, phone Traveline on **0800 464 00 00** or visit **www.traveline.cymru**

Leave gates and property as you find them – follow paths unless wider access is available

» A farmer will normally close gates to keep farm animals in, but may sometimes leave them open so the animals can reach food and water. Leave gates as you find them or follow instructions on signs. When in a group, make sure the last person knows how to leave the gates.

» Follow paths unless wider access is available, such as on open country or registered common land (known as 'open access' land).

» If you think a sign is illegal or misleading such as a *Private – No Entry* sign on a public path, contact the local authority.

» Leave machinery and farm animals alone – don't interfere with animals even if you think they're in distress. Try to alert the farmer instead.

» Use gates, stiles or gaps in field boundaries if you can – climbing over walls, hedges and fences can damage them and increase the risk of farm animals escaping.

» Our heritage matters to all of us – be careful not to disturb ruins and historic sites.

PROTECT THE NATURAL ENVIRONMENT

We all have a responsibility to protect the countryside now and for future generations, so make sure you don't harm animals, birds, plants or trees and try to leave no trace of your visit. When out with your dog make sure it is not a danger or nuisance to farm animals, horses, wildlife or other people.

Leave no trace of your visit and take your litter home

» Protecting the natural environment means taking special care not to damage, destroy or remove features such as rocks, plants and trees. They provide homes and food for wildlife, and add to everybody's enjoyment of the countryside.

» Litter and leftover food doesn't just spoil the beauty of the countryside, it can be dangerous to wildlife and farm animals – so take your litter home with you. Dropping litter and dumping rubbish are criminal offences.

» Fires can be as devastating to wildlife and habitats as they are to people and property – so be careful with naked flames and cigarettes at any time of the year. Sometimes, controlled fires are used to manage vegetation, particularly on heaths and moors between 1 October and 15 April, but if a fire appears to be unattended then report it by calling **999**.

Keep dogs under effective control

When you take your dog into the outdoors, always ensure it does not disturb wildlife, farm animals, horses or other people by keeping it under effective control. This means that you:

» keep your dog on a lead, or

» keep it in sight at all times, be aware of what it's doing and be confident it will return to you promptly on command

» ensure it does not stray off the path or area where you have a right of access

Special dog rules may apply in particular situations, so always look out for local signs – for example:

» dogs may be banned from certain areas that people use, or there may be restrictions, byelaws or control orders limiting where they can go

» the access rights that normally apply to open country and registered common land (known as 'open access' land) require dogs to be kept on a short lead between 1 March and 31 July, to help protect ground-nesting birds, and all year round near farm animals

» at the coast, there may also be some local restrictions to require dogs to be kept on a short lead during the bird breeding season, and to prevent disturbance to flocks of resting and feeding birds during other times of year

It's always good practice (and a legal requirement on 'open access' land) to keep your dog on a lead around farm animals and horses, for your own safety and for the welfare of the animals. A farmer may shoot a dog which is attacking or chasing farm animals without being liable to compensate the dog's owner.

However, if cattle or horses chase you and your dog, it is safer to let your dog off the lead – don't risk getting hurt by trying to protect it. Your dog will be much safer if you let it run away from a farm animal in these circumstances and so will you.

Everyone knows how unpleasant dog mess is and it can cause infections, so always clean up after your dog and get rid of the mess responsibly – 'bag it and bin it'. Make sure your dog is wormed regularly to protect it, other animals and people.

ENJOY THE OUTDOORS

Even when going out locally, it's best to get the latest information about where and when you can go. For example, your rights to go on to some areas of open access land and coastal land may be restricted in particular places at particular times. Find out as much as you can about where you are going, plan ahead and follow advice and local signs.

Plan ahead and be prepared

You'll get more from your visit if you refer to up-to-date maps or guidebooks and websites before you go. Visit **naturalresources.wales** or contact local information centres or libraries for a list of outdoor recreation groups offering advice on specialist activities.

You're responsible for your own safety and for others in your care – especially children – so be prepared for natural hazards, changes in weather and other events. Wild animals, farm animals and horses can behave unpredictably if you get too close, especially if they're with their young – so give them plenty of space.

Check weather forecasts before you leave. Conditions can change rapidly especially on mountains and along the coast, so don't be afraid to turn back. When visiting the coast check for tide times on **www.ukho.gov.uk/easytide** – don't risk getting cut off by rising tides and take care on slippery rocks and seaweed.

Part of the appeal of the countryside is that you can get away from it all. You may not see anyone for hours, and there are many places without clear mobile phone signals, so let someone else know where you're going and when you expect to return.

Follow advice and local signs

Wales has about 33,000 kilometres (20,750 miles) of public rights of way, providing many opportunities to enjoy the natural environment. Get to know the signs and symbols used in the countryside to show paths and open countryside.

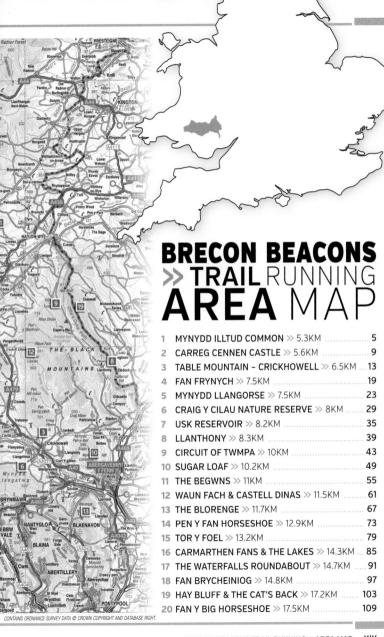

BRECON BEACONS
›› TRAIL RUNNING
AREA MAP

CONTAINS ORDNANCE SURVEY DATA © CROWN COPYRIGHT AND DATABASE RIGHT.

THE
TRAILS

We have spent many happy hours choosing our favourite off-road routes in the Brecon Beacons with the aim of showing you the best trails, views and landscapes that the area has to offer. In this selection, there should be something for everyone: easier runs on peaceful common land or around lakeshore; moderate to tough fell runs in the mountains, immersing you in the region's varied terrain; and longer, more challenging circuits taking in the superb ridges, summits, escarpments and waterfalls of the national park. Apologies if we have not included your own favourite; we have chosen twenty and could have included many more!

Be prepared for rain, mist, bog and mud – this is Wales! But when the skies are blue, the mountains are glowing in the afternoon sun and a red kite is wheeling and mewing overhead, you won't wish to be running anywhere else in the world.

JEN SCOTNEY AND JON DREVER ON THE DRAGON'S BACK RIDGE (RUN 12).

THE STUNNING BACKDROP TO THE FINAL DESCENT OF THE CARMARTHEN FANS ROUTE [RUN 16].

JON DREVER AND TRACY PURNELL ON MYNYDD ILLTUD COMMON.

INTRODUCTION

This is an easy and beautiful run on the common land around the national park visitor centre. While short in distance, it packs in spectacular, far-reaching views, and the terrace outside the excellent tearooms is an inviting place to refuel afterwards. The route visits the remains of an Iron Age hill fort sitting atop the grassy mound of Twyn y Gaer. It's easy to see why our ancestors picked this natural defensive spot to settle – there are huge, widescreen views towards Pen y Fan and Corn Du, while the northern slopes of the Black Mountains and the snaking River Usk are also visible.

Mynydd Illtud is one of several commons purchased by the National Park Authority to conserve the open landscape. These are a remnant of the medieval manorial system where crops were grown on areas with better soil, and the poorer land was used for grazing and local people had rights to use the common land. Commoners' rights are unchanged today, while visitors can enjoy an abundance of wildlife, such as red kites, larks, wheatears and colourful butterflies.

For keen runners, staff in the centre will show you other routes that can easily be tagged on to this one, perhaps venturing to the nearby nature reserve of Traeth Mawr or on to neighbouring Cefn Llechid common.

THE ROUTE

From the visitor centre you follow easy tracks over open common, enjoying superb views of the mountains. A short climb on a grassy hillside brings you to the ancient hill fort and trig point with 360-degree views. From here there is a lovely descent before following the boundary of the common back to the start.

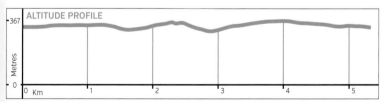

ALTITUDE PROFILE

Metres

367

0

Km   1   2   3   4   5

» MYNYDD ILLTUD COMMON

DISTANCE 5.3KM » *ASCENT* 100M » *MAX ALTITUDE* 367M » *TYPICAL TIME* 0:40 HRS » *TERRAIN* GOOD TRACKS ON OPEN COMMON LAND » *NAVIGATION* 1 – EASY » *START/FINISH PAY* CAR PARK AT BRECON BEACONS NATIONAL PARK VISITOR CENTRE, LIBANUS » *GRID REF* SN 978263 » *SATNAV* LD3 8ER » *OS MAP* EXPLORER OL12 BRECON BEACONS NATIONAL PARK WESTERN AREA, OR LANDRANGER 160 BRECON BEACONS » *REFRESHMENTS* TEAROOMS IN VISITOR CENTRE.

S Go through the gate at the far (north-east) end of the car park on to the common. There are several paths radiating out from here, but take the widest one that continues **straight ahead**, parallel with the fence to the right. On the right, there are exceptional views of Pen y Fan and ahead to the Black Mountains. **Ignore** any paths off to the left and right. The track goes through an area of gorse and eventually passes to the left of a small marshy pond. Soon after, the track emerges on to a clearing and meets a minor tarmac road. Ahead to the left you can see the hill of Twyn y Gaer and its trig pillar.

2 Cross the road and follow the path to the left of the fence, descending to another minor road.

3 Cross the road and take the grassy path that climbs ahead and up the **right-hand side** of the hill to the Iron Age fort and trig pillar. Make a note of the other track to the left, on which you will descend. Remains of ditches are still evident around the summit and you can look down into the Usk Valley as well as enjoy superb mountain views.

4 You can vary your route back by taking the path to the right of your ascent, which is almost directly south and looks towards Pen y Fan from the top. After 50m from the trig pillar, you cross a track and shortly after this the path splits, both options dropping down the hillside. Take the track **on the right** that descends towards the left of some trees and crosses a stream before reaching the road.

5 Cross the road to a signpost. Follow the bridleway sign for the *Mountain Centre* but after about 10m the path forks. Here **fork right** to join a track next to the fence. Follow the wall/fence boundary of the common all the way around until eventually you meet a farm access track just after passing a small pond on your left. (You can also cut across the common, back to the Mountain Centre at any point.)

6 **Turn left** on to the farm access track then cross the road and **continue ahead**. At a large stone, **take the left fork** to follow a path the short distance back to the start.

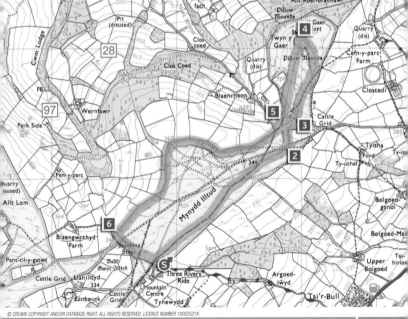

HEADING OUT PAST THE CASTLE.

INTRODUCTION

Perched on a 91-metre-high exposed limestone crag, Carreg Cennen is everyone's idea of how a ruined castle should look. It even has an underground passage, dug from the rock, leading down into a cave. The ruins are believed to date from the 12th or 13th century, although an earlier castle probably predated this. Carreg Cennen was also the original finish of the legendary Dragon's Back Race, making a spectacular end for the gruelling 315-kilometre run from Conwy Castle down the mountainous spine of Wales. Starting at the castle, our run is an easy-to-follow, hilly circuit with superb views of the ruins – one of the Brecon Beacons' most memorable landmarks – for much of the route.

THE ROUTE

A lovely descent through oak woodlands leads to a crossing of the Afon Cennen. The route then curves around the facing hillside through porous limestone country, before recrossing the river and climbing back up to the castle on its rocky perch. This route is one of the waymarked walks from the castle and is signed with red 'castle' markers.

NOTE: You don't have to pay the castle entrance fee if you are just doing this run and not visiting the ruins.

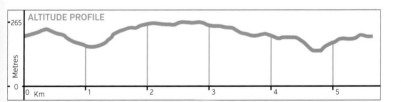

ALTITUDE PROFILE

» CARREG CENNEN CASTLE

DISTANCE 5.6KM » *ASCENT* 200M » *MAX ALTITUDE* 265M » *TYPICAL TIME* 0:50 HRS » *TERRAIN* MAINLY CLEAR PATHS IN WOODLAND AND PASTURE. SHORT SECTION OF ROAD AND GRAVEL TRACK » *NAVIGATION* 1 – ROUTE SIGNPOSTED AS A WALK (RED CASTLE SIGNS) » *START/FINISH* CAR PARK AT CARREG CENNEN CASTLE. CHECK *WWW.CARREGCENNENCASTLE.COM* FOR CASTLE AND CAR PARK OPENING TIMES » *GRID REFERENCE* SN 666193 » *SATNAV* SA19 6UA » *OS MAP* EXPLORERS OL12 BRECON BEACONS NATIONAL PARK WESTERN AREA, 186 LLANDEILO & BRECHFA FOREST, 178 LLANELLI & AMMANFORD; OR LANDRANGER 159 SWANSEA & GOWER » *REFRESHMENTS* TEAROOMS AT CASTLE.

DIRECTIONS » CARREG CENNEN CASTLE

S From the car park go past the tearooms and through a wooden gate to climb the path towards the castle. It **veers left** below the rocky bluff and comes to the castle entrance where there is a payment booth (**you don't have to pay if you're just doing this route and not visiting the castle**). Continue **straight ahead** through the wooden gate to the far left of the booth. A lovely path slants downhill through the oak wood to bring you to the river and the bottom of the valley.

2 Cross the footbridge and then, soon afterwards, a second footbridge to continue uphill through woodland on a broad path. Cross a stile on to a farm track. Here, **bear left** and take the track zigzagging uphill. It almost immediately bends sharp right and, a little later on, bends back to the left. **Do not** take the left-hand bend, but continue **straight ahead** on to another track, staying on the Beacons Way. At the top of the climb cross a stile between two gates and follow the path along the edge of the fields (staying on the Beacons Way and ignoring a gate on the left into a field). The path **curves to the left** and eventually you join a track to continue past the barns and farm at Brondai to reach a road.

3 **Turn right** and follow the road through a quiet valley, crossing a cattle grid. After about 400m, **turn right** to follow a footpath over a stile and cross to the top left corner of the field. The path turns **sharp left** and drops down another field. It soon becomes a track, descending alongside the river until you reach a metal gate. Cross the stile to pass through a marshy area and follow the track through fields until you come to a T-junction with another track. **Turn right** here, heading downhill. Cross a cattle grid and ford a stream and continue along the track until you reach a house where the track forks.

4 **Fork left** (the right fork continues ahead into the grounds of the property) to follow a path descending steeply down a field. At the bottom, cross a stile and a footbridge, before climbing a steep bank and passing two houses to reach a gate on to a road.

5 **Turn left** and head up the road for about 300m. Look out for a signpost **on the right** showing a footpath across the field. Here, go through the gate and follow the path, aiming for a gate to the left of the buildings below the castle. This brings you to the tearooms where you can track back to the car park.

JOHN PRICE ON THE FINAL FEW STEPS TO THE SUMMIT OF TABLE MOUNTAIN.

03 » TABLE MOUNTAIN – CRICKHOWELL   6.5km

INTRODUCTION

Crickhowell is a small picturesque market town in the Usk Valley with independent shops, restaurants and inns. It lies on the southern edge of the Black Mountains – with the Brecon Beacons just across and up the valley. The flat-topped Table Mountain dominates the view to the north and on its unusually shaped summit lies the Crug Hywel Iron Age fort from which the town takes its name.

This run is short but delightful – and is perfect for a before-breakfast excursion or a leisurely evening outing. The view from the top encompasses the whole of the Usk Valley with the Brecon Beacons range beyond.

For those with a desire to 'bag a trig point', the run can be extended to take in Pen Cerrig-calch (and Pen Allt-mawr beyond) to experience the most westerly ridge of the Black Mountains before returning to Table Mountain and thence descending to Crickhowell.

THE ROUTE

The route starts up a quiet tarmac lane before ascending through fields and a wooded path before reaching the open hillside, after which an undulating path takes you to the top of the mountain. The descent is initially via fields, then a short section of road followed by a bridleway to return to the starting point.

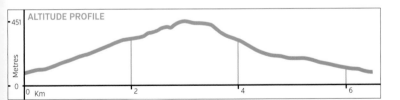

>> **TABLE MOUNTAIN – CRICKHOWELL**

DISTANCE 6.5KM » *ASCENT* 360M » *MAX ALTITUDE* 451M » *TYPICAL TIME* 1:00–1:30 HRS » *TERRAIN* VARIOUS – FIELDS, WOODS, OPEN HILLSIDE, SHORT ROAD SECTIONS. GOOD PATHS – MAINLY GRASSY, BUT WITH ROCKY SECTIONS AND MUDDY IN PLACES » *NAVIGATION* **2** – BASIC SKILLS REQUIRED » *START/FINISH* FROM A40 ROAD AT WESTERN EDGE OF TOWN. STREET PARKING AND CAR PARK IN CRICKHOWELL » *GRID REF* SO 214190 » *SATNAV* NP8 1SE » *OS MAP* EXPLORER OL13 BRECON BEACONS NATIONAL PARK EASTERN AREA, OR LANDRANGER 161 THE BLACK MOUNTAINS » *TRANSPORT* BUSES STOP AT CRICKHOWELL FROM EITHER BRECON OR ABERGAVENNY » *REFRESHMENTS* NUMEROUS OPTIONS IN CRICKHOWELL.

DIRECTIONS >> TABLE MOUNTAIN – CRICKHOWELL

S The run begins from the quaint wooden shelter on the main A40 at the western edge of the town. This shelter is on the right, some 200m beyond the third zebra crossing heading out of Crickhowell (Everest Drive on the left), and just before the Red Indigo restaurant. Take the (un-named) road up the hill for approximately 400m before **turning right** down a walled path (signposted *Table Mountain and Beacons Way*). After crossing a pretty bridge climb 100m to a fingerpost and stile **on the left** (just before a set of double metal gates).

2 Go over the stile and through the stables and follow the path uphill through three fields with the Cumbeth dingle and stream below to your left. Cross a small stream and go through a gate into the woods and continue onwards and upwards (**ignoring** the side paths to the left and the right). The path eventually reaches a gate by a stream. Cross the stream and continue up the right-hand edge of the field to where the path goes between stone walls (and initially shares a short section of the stream) before reaching a walled sheepfold – pass through two gates and reach the open hillside.

3 **Turn right** and climb the path (rocky in parts) keeping the wall and fence to the right. There are a number of short steep ascents and numerous crossings of small streams before the path begins to level out as it curves round to the right towards the (now very distinctive) Table Mountain. The final ascent requires picking a way through a rocky jumble but the view from the top is spectacular – although the 'table' slopes somewhat!

OPTIONAL ROUTE TO PEN CARRIG-CALCH AND/OR PEN ALLT-MAWR [NOT ON MAP] (Adds 3/7km, *c.*240m ascent, 0:45/1:00–1:15/1:45 hrs. A compass and map are required in poor visibility.)

OR If you wish to take in the tops of Pen Cerrig-calch and/or Pen Allt-mawr beyond, retrace your steps to the col immediately north of Table Mountain and take the obvious (initially wide and grassy but increasingly rocky) path up the broad ridge (north-westerly) to ultimately reach the Pen Cerrig-calch trig point. The trig point at Pen Allt-mawr (somewhat the worse for wear – but another wonderful viewpoint) is another 2km further along the relatively flat but stony ridge path. »

4 The descent from Table Mountain can be direct down a steep rocky path from the southern edge of the escarpment or via the fort's old entrance on the eastern edge (directly opposite the Sugar Loaf): after proceeding through the old gateway (now merely a gap in the earth bank), the main path swings initially left and then you should take the grassy path leading down to the right which curves around the lower slopes of the hillside. Both paths meet at a gate/stile (south of the top).

5 Leave the open hillside via the gate/stile which leads on to a short rocky lane. Exit the lane via the first stile **on the left** and go down the left-hand edge of a field, through a gate/stile. Towards the end of the next track **go right** through a metal gate (signed *Beacons Way*). Continue down the left-hand edge of several fields (via stiles and gate) to then join a path/lane leading **half left** between hedges. The lane exits via a stile and **left** into a field (with a small stream alongside). Just before the bottom left corner of the field, the path passes through a gap in the hedge by the stream and reaches the Crickhowell to Llanbedr road via the farmyard of Ty-yn-y-wlad.

6 **Turn right** for a short (300m) section on the road and take the second track **to the right** just after a gate (also on the right). Follow this (**ignoring** all paths off) descending until you reach the bridge and walled lane up which you came originally. On reaching the metalled road, **turn left** and descend to the main A40 and the starting point.

GREAT SINGLETRACK IN THE UPPER SECTION OF CWM CUMBETH.

EASY RUNNING ALONG SARN HELEN.

04 >> FAN FRYNYCH

7.5km

INTRODUCTION

A few hundred metres from the busy A470 and the crowds on Pen y Fan is a hidden gem, the national nature reserve at Fan Frynych, a quiet area of the national park with a different character to the rest of the central Brecon Beacons. With wonderful panoramic views, the peak of Fan Frynych is the focus of this circuit and marks the northernmost ridge of Fforest Fawr – the Great Forest – once a royal hunting ground.

Initially you follow Sarn Helen, a Roman road which once linked Neath and Brecon. After the Roman Empire fell, this continued to be an important route for many centuries, used by drovers to take livestock to market.

The most impressive features of the reserve are the north-facing precipitous crags of Craig Cerrig-gleisiad and Craig

Cwm-du. The descent from Fan Frynych provides glimpses into Craig Cerrig-gleisiad, which is steep-sided woodland, with trees and shrubs clinging to the cliffs and home to rare alpine plants and birdlife, including peregrines, kestrel, red grouse, red kites and rare ring ouzels.

THE ROUTE

An easy approach of three kilometres along Sarn Helen, beneath the ridge of Fan Frynych, leads you to an old drovers road, which you follow to climb the lower slopes of the hill. A straightforward ascent on grassy, open slopes brings you to the summit of Fan Frynych for superb views of the central Brecon Beacons. From here it's a fun, fast descent on good tracks back to the start.

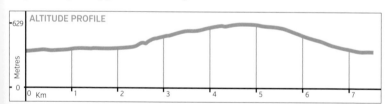

ALTITUDE PROFILE

>> FAN FRYNYCH

DISTANCE 7.5KM >> *ASCENT* 270M >> *MAX ALTITUDE* 629M >> *TYPICAL TIME* 1:00–1:30 HRS >> *TERRAIN* VARIED – GRAVEL TRACK, GOOD PATHS AND TRACK, INDISTINCT IN PLACES, MOSTLY GRASSY OR HARD PACKED >> *NAVIGATION* 3 – PATH INDISTINCT IN PLACES ON THE OPEN SLOPES UP TO THE TRIG PILLAR. MAP AND COMPASS NEEDED IN POOR WEATHER AS IT'S EASY TO LOSE THE PATH TO THE SUMMIT >> *START/FINISH* LAY-BY NEAR FOREST LODGE FARMHOUSE AND COTTAGES >> *SATNAV* LD3 8NW >> *GRID REF* SN 961241 >> *OS MAP* EXPLORER OL12 BRECON BEACONS NATIONAL PARK WESTERN AREA, OR LANDRANGER 160 BRECON BEACONS >> *REFRESHMENTS* TAI'R BULL COUNTRY INN, LIBANUS; TEAROOMS AT NATIONAL PARK VISITOR CENTRE.

DIRECTIONS >> FAN FRYNYCH

S   From the right-angled junction at Forest Lodge Cottages, take the track south-west and through a gate with a *Motorised vehicles are prohibited* sign. Continue to a second gate and cattle grid where a track leaves to the left (signposted *Twyn Dylluan-ddu*). Make a note that this is your return route from the ridge on the left. The straight gravel track ahead is Sarn Helen. Follow this for roughly 2km, passing through two more gates/cattle grids. Not long after the end of the forest plantation on your right you reach a metal gate to the left of the track. Here the track divides: the left fork is a grassy track (an old drovers road) that passes through the gate and towards the trees on the skyline, while the right fork continues along Sarn Helen.

2   **Take the left fork** which climbs gently to the wind-twisted trees then curves around **to the left** to continue uphill. There are great views of Sarn Helen, snaking its way south, and the western Fans in the distance. At the top the path **turns sharp left** while straight ahead are views of steep cliffs towering above the Craig Cwm-du valley.

3   Follow the path **sharp left** to climb the slopes of Fan Frynych, heading towards a cairn on the skyline. The path is indistinct in places, crossing boggy, featureless slopes: in poor weather it would be easy to lose your way here. Continue on the path, passing to the left of the cairn (where a path joins from the Craig Cwm-du valley), until you reach the trig pillar at the summit. Take in the superb views of the central Brecon Beacons ahead and dramatic cliffs of Craig Cerrig-gleisiad to the right.

4   From the trig pillar, take the middle of three paths, to the right of the lake and heading roughly east. This path meets a wider stony path, where you **turn left** and continue along the ridge passing close to small quarry spoils. This path drops down to the hill fence where it joins a wide track from the right and continues through a gate and then falls to a junction with two gates and a stile. (Alternatively, from the trig pillar you can continue on the path roughly east until you meet the hill fence and here **turn left** on to a wide track which drops to the same gate.)

5   **Turn sharp left** and follow the clear track down to Sarn Helen. **Turn right** to return to the start.

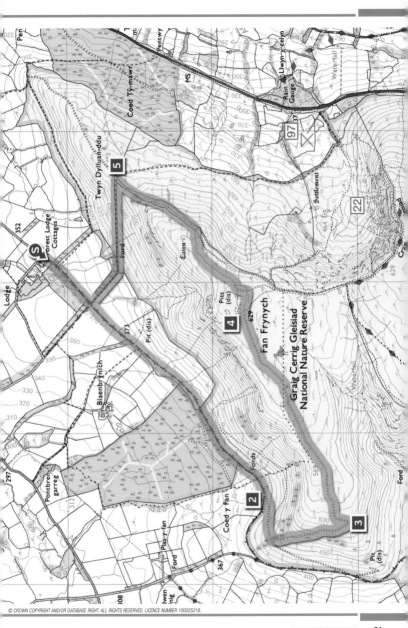

TRACY PURNELL AND JEN SCOTNEY ON COCKIT HILL.

INTRODUCTION

Llangors Lake is the largest natural lake in South Wales, known for its fishing and watersports. Overlooking it is Mynydd Llangorse and this lovely circuit of the peak starts from the col between the hill and its distinctive neighbour, Mynydd Troed.

This run is all about the views. The first half leads you down a delightful valley, followed by open moorland with a spectacular 360-degree panorama that includes the Black Mountains, topped by the distinctive ridge of Pen Allt-mawr. The main Beacons range lies to the west and the lake glistens below as you enjoy a superb descent of Cockit Hill to return to the start.

For those with the energy, there is an option to extend this route by climbing to the Mynydd Troed trig pillar on the opposite side of the col.

THE ROUTE

From the car park it's a gradual descent on an often muddy path down Cwm Sorgwm under the Cockit Hill ridge. A stiff climb takes you on to the ridge, followed by a flattish wide green path skirting under the broad Mynydd Llangorse ridge. It's a grassy, open ride to the trig pillar then a gently undulating track – with the odd rocky section but mainly wide and grassy – along the ridge before a wonderful 'flat-out' descent back to the car. If you're still feeling fresh, a 'straight-up-and-down', two-kilometre optional extension takes in Mynydd Troed from the col.

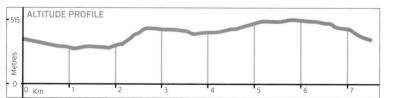

ALTITUDE PROFILE

» MYNYDD LLANGORSE

DISTANCE 7.5KM » *ASCENT* 270M » *MAX ALTITUDE* 515M » *TYPICAL TIME* 1:00–1:30 HRS » *TERRAIN* VARIOUS – OPEN HILLSIDE, GOOD PATHS (GRASSY, SOME ROCKY AND BOGGY) » *NAVIGATION* 3 – EASY IN CLEAR WEATHER. FROM POINT 3 TO THE TRIG PILLAR AT 6 WOULD BE TRICKY IN MIST » *START/FINISH* SMALL PARKING AREA AT COL BETWEEN MYNYDD TROED AND MYNYDD LLANGORSE, ON MINOR ROAD FROM LLANGORS TO WAUN FACH VIA CWM SORGWM » *GRID REF* SO 160283 » *SATNAV* LD3 7UL (NEAREST) *OS MAP* EXPLORER OL13 BRECON BEACONS NATIONAL PARK EASTERN AREA, OR LANDRANGER 161 THE BLACK MOUNTAINS » *REFRESHMENTS* OPTIONS IN TALGARTH AND LLANGORSE.

S From the car park take the path (initially hidden amongst the gorse bushes – to the left when looking up the broad slope of Cockit Hill) that skirts under the ridge of the hill and down the Cwm Sorgwm valley (starting above the road and gradually moving away from it). This path starts as a narrow (often muddy) gully between gorse bushes and bracken, but gradually opens up after roughly 1km. Follow it for approximately 2km (gently descending and crossing some small streams) and occasionally meeting (but staying above) the hill intake fence. Cockit Hill ridge is above to the right and there are splendid views ahead and left down Cwm Sorgwm towards Waun Fach and Cwmdu. As occasional paths go off left, take the right and higher forks.

2 The path forks approximately 200m before a line of oak trees – take the **right fork**, gently uphill through bracken, up to the corner of a fence. (If the bracken is too high for comfort, continue on the left-hand path to a gate: **don't** go through it, but **turn right** and follow outside the fence to the fence corner.) At the fence corner, cross a small stream and follow the (often muddy) path steeply and diagonally uphill. One sharp right zig halfway up followed by a left zag to eventually emerge on a wide grassy slope from where the path leads to a large cairn (where views open up of the Usk valley above Crickhowell with Mynydd Llangatwg beyond).

3 Pass **to the right** of the cairn and soon after this **turn right** at a fingerpost to join a wide grassy ride climbing gently uphill. After approx 200m (just before a lone tree) take a grassy path off **to the left**: follow this path (mainly flat) for approximately 1km skirting above Blaen-y-cwm as views open up left across to the Pen Tir ridge and the 'tower' at Tretower beyond and down the valley.

4 Where a slightly wider and more used track joins from the right, **turn sharp right** uphill – heading now for the broad, flat top of Mynydd Llangorse. Continue for approximately 500m.

5 At a low broken earth bank on the left, take a slightly smaller path **left** uphill – still heading for the top of Mynydd Llangorse. After some gentle rises the path reaches the trig pillar. ≫

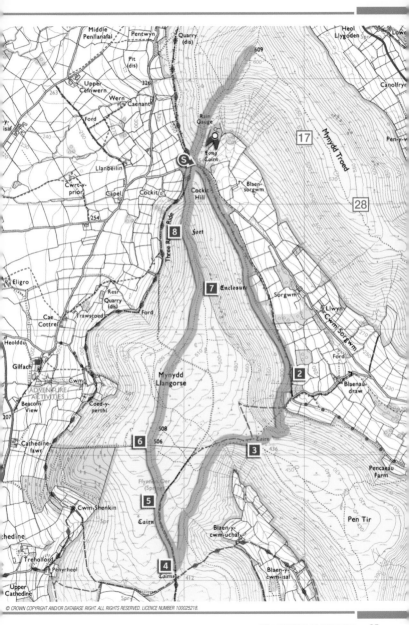

6   Continue north along the obvious ridge track/path for approximately 1km. Views begin to open up on the left of the upper Wye Valley, the Brecon Beacons and, eventually, Llangors Lake (below left), with the most eastern ridges of the Black Mountains on the right (Waun Fach and the Pen Cerrig-calch/Pen Allt-mawr ridge).

7   After passing a prominent isolated boulder the path **veers left** and begins to descend. The path splits up here, but all branches eventually merge together in approx. 400m. The ridge begins to narrow (if concerned about exposure stay to the left) and ends at a small rocky outcrop.

8   From the rocky outcrop the car can be seen below (hopefully!) and the way home is a flat-out sprint down a wide grassy slope (with a rocky zigzag path to the right of the slope for the more cautious).

OPTIONAL ROUTE: MYNYDD TROED
(Adds 2km, 250m ascent, 0:30–0:45 hrs.)

Those still feeling fresh can take the 'up-and-back-down' optional extension to the trig pillar on Mynydd Troed. Go through the gate opposite the descent from Mynydd Llangorse and take the obvious path **straight up** the hillside (how far can you keep running?). After a series of 'steps' approximately halfway up, the path emerges on to an old rocky track. From here either cross the track and continue on the path still heading steeply and directly to the summit – or follow the track **right** and then **veer left** for a more gentle ascent (both end at the trig point). Descend the way you have come up (but probably a little more quickly!).

LOOKING AHEAD FROM COCKIT HILL TO MYNYDD TROED.

INTRODUCTION

Perched high on the hills above the Usk Valley, Craig y Cilau is the sweeping amphitheatre of cliffs and screes that curl around the northern edge of Mynydd Llangatwg. This is one of the largest limestone cliffs in South Wales and the nature reserve has a markedly different character to the rest of the national park. This route takes in the best of the location, while a lovely path along the high-level tramway from its quarrying past gives superb views across to the Black Mountains. The area is now a cavers' paradise, and the run passes near to the old (now sealed) entrance to the famous Ogof Agen Allwedd (known locally as 'Aggy') system, with over 30 kilometres of surveyed passageways.

THE ROUTE

The track out is flat, but then it's a stiff climb on an old quarry incline to a clearing with great views of the Black Mountains. A steep path up an open hillside on an old quarry track brings you to a dramatic terrace running below the cliffs. Contour along here, before dropping back into the valley and then up to the bog of Waun Ddu. After crossing the Llangattock/Beaufort road, you descend to a river and follow the fields back to Llangattock.

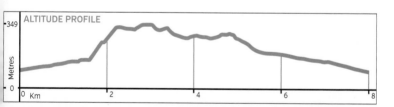

ALTITUDE PROFILE

» CRAIG Y CILAU NATURE RESERVE

DISTANCE 8KM » **ASCENT** 340M » **MAX ALTITUDE** 349M » **TYPICAL TIME** 1:15–1:30 HRS » **TERRAIN** MOSTLY GOOD PATHS AND ONE SHORT ROAD SECTION. CAN BE MUDDY IN WET CONDITIONS » **NAVIGATION 2** – PATH ON SECOND HALF OF CLIMB BETWEEN POINTS 3 AND 4 CAN BE HIDDEN BY BRACKEN IN SUMMER » **START/FINISH** BEND IN MINOR ROAD NEAR LLANGATTOCK – PARKING AVAILABLE IN VILLAGE OR LAY-BY NEAR CANAL BRIDGE » **GRID REF** SO 208174 » **SATNAV** NP8 1LD » **OS MAP** EXPLORER OL13 BRECON BEACONS NATIONAL PARK EASTERN AREA, OR LANDRANGER 161 THE BLACK MOUNTAINS » **REFRESHMENTS** VINE TREE PUB, LLANGATTOCK; PLENTY OF OPTIONS IN CRICKHOWELL.

S   Start in Llangattock village. Follow a minor road south-west out of the village, crossing the canal bridge, until you reach a sharp bend left.

2   At this bend, just before the footpath sign, **turn right** through a metal gate. Follow a wide track that **swings left**, passing through another gate. This section can be very muddy! **Continue ahead**, **ignoring** a stile to the left, and through another gate. Follow the track, passing into an open field – stay on the right-hand edge along the old tramway and to the right of Cwm Bach Farm. Cross a stream to reach a stile in the bottom right corner of the field.

3   Cross the stile (but reaching it could involve wet feet!) and over a wide track. Straight ahead is a very steep, stony track on the right of a fence and woodland. Go **straight up** here for 250m. At the top reach a clearing at the end of the woods. Behind you are superb views to Table Mountain and the Black Mountains. Just to the right is a welcome seat (you will probably be in need of this by now!). From the clearing, take the path climbing **diagonally left** up the hillside to reach a grassy terrace below crags.

4   **Turn right** on to the path below the crags, passing a visitor information board. Continue round the terrace in a long, sweeping arc initially west, then south-west and north-west, passing a memorial, until you reach a waymarked fork in the path. The path right descends into the valley. (You can take a short side trip here by taking the left fork to continue to the end of the terrace to see the Agen Allwedd cave entrance, but it is sealed off – and entry into this seemingly uninviting hole is surely not for sensible trail runners!)

5   **Fork right** to drop into the valley until you reach a fork at a waymarked post. Follow the yellow arrow **to the right**, descending steeply through bracken and hawthorn trees to reach a path junction at the valley base. »

6   **Turn left** to head up the valley, climbing slightly and then descending alongside an old wall on the right. At the sharp right bend in the wall, continue **straight ahead** towards the obvious bog, Waun Ddu. Skirt the bog on the **left-hand side**, passing through an impressive collection of boulders, and then climb to the *National Nature Reserve* sign. Continue **ahead** until you meet a track.

7   **Turn left** on to the track and drop to a road. **Cross with care** and take the path directly **ahead**, dropping steeply to cross a stile into a field. Descend across the field diagonally to a gate in the bottom right corner. Go through the gate into the woods. **Turn right** and follow a track through the woods, until you reach a field. Here **turn left** and follow a path along the edge of the woods, dropping steeply down to the river.

8   **Do not** cross the river, but instead **turn right** and follow a track along the left-hand edge of a field. Continue with Coed y Cilau woods to your left, through several fields, crossing various stiles, to join a track leading to Cilau Farm.

9   As you approach the farm buildings, **ignore** the footpath sign pointing left (which drops down to the river). Instead head to a stile on the far right-hand side of the field, at the end of the cowshed, between two metal gates. Cross the stile and continue past the farm to the bottom left-hand corner of the field where you reach a stile.

10   Cross the stile and **turn left** on to a lane. Where it bends left, **turn immediately right** into a field. (Notice the 'catapult' tree on the left!) Continue to the stile at the end. Cross the stile and after crossing straight over one last field **turn left** on to a road. This takes you over a canal bridge and back to Llangattock village.

THE VIEW AHEAD TOWARDS WAUN DDU.

FAST RUNNING ON THE LAKESIDE TRAIL AROUND USK RESERVOIR.

07 >> **USK RESERVOIR**   8.2km

INTRODUCTION

The setting of the Usk Reservoir is picturesque and tranquil, high in the remote and wild foothills of the Black Mountain (Mynydd Du) range, with tantalising glimpses of the mountains through the trees. This undulating circuit of the reservoir uses a waymarked cycling and walking loop. It is easy to follow and offers excellent views of forest, lake, mountains and the surrounding moorland.

THE ROUTE

This run goes all the way around the reservoir and is undulating, with both short and longer climbs. It is run anticlockwise so there are fewer choices of path to confuse at the beginning. Leaving the parking area, you cross the dam wall and then follow a short stretch of road before picking up the lakeside forest trail. This climbs and falls through woodland and open hillside, around the water's edge, to the head of the reservoir, where you cross a stream and then climb up above the lake. You drop into a small valley and then turn away from the water, following forestry paths back to the start.

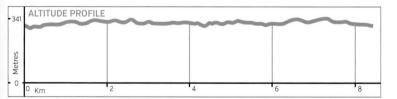

ALTITUDE PROFILE

341

Metres

0

0   Km   2   4   6   8

>> **USK RESERVOIR**

DISTANCE 8.2KM >> *ASCENT* 180M >> *MAX ALTITUDE* 341M >> *TYPICAL TIME* 1:00–1:30 HRS
>> *TERRAIN* GOOD FOREST TRAILS, SOME TARMAC ROAD >> *NAVIGATION 1* – STRAIGHTFORWARD
START/FINISH PARKING AREA BY RESERVOR DAM. THE RESERVOIR IS 10KM FROM TRECASTLE AND
SIGNPOSTED ON THE LLANDDEUSANT ROAD >> *GRID REF* SN 833286 >> *SATNAV* LD3 8YF
(NEAREST) >> *OS MAP* EXPLORER OL12 BRECON BEACONS NATONAL PARK WESTERN AREA, OR
LANDRANGER 160 BRECON BEACONS >> *REFRESHMENTS* CASTLE COACHING INN, TRECASTLE.

DIRECTIONS ≫ USK RESERVOIR

S From the parking area, cross the dam wall and **turn left** on to a road. Follow this for roughly 800m to a small parking area, where the road ends.

2 **Ignore** the track straight ahead, which leads to a reservoir building. Take the forestry track **to your right**, bypassing a metal barrier, and follow this uphill for roughly 50m, before **taking a left fork** on to the lakeside path. To the left are great views of the reservoir and mountains. The path rises and falls through the woodland before eventually reaching an open area where it turns **sharp left** at the end of the reservoir.

3 After 10m, cross a footbridge then continue around the open hillside. The path climbs steeply, then drops and turns away from the water into woodland and then drops steeply through a small valley. Cross a footbridge and then climb the hill (**ignoring** a clearing to the left) and continue ahead, to then descend to a junction with a track on the left.

4 **Turn left**. This track climbs through the forest until you meet a junction with a signpost.

5 **Turn left** following the mountain bike signs. The track drops gently until you meet a track crossing in front of you.

6 **Turn right** and follow this until it meets a tarmac road (with a metal barrier).

7 **Turn left** on to the road. Follow this back to the parking area, **ignoring** a wide track to the left that takes you to the water.

JEN SCOTNEY AND JON BARTON CLIMBING ABOVE LLANTHONY PRIORY.

08 » LLANTHONY

8.3km

INTRODUCTION

The beautiful and evocative ruins of Llanthony Priory lie in the Vale of Ewyas, beneath the Black Mountains. It was founded in the 12th century by Norman nobleman William de Lacy and was home to a community of Augustinian monks. Today, the remains are all that survive of what was once one of the greatest buildings in medieval Wales. In its heyday, live fish were transported from Llangors Lake along the Rhiw Pyscod for the monastery fishponds, while another path, Rhiw Cwrw, was built to bring the monks beer from Abbeydore.

On this circuit, the first two-kilometre climb to the Hatterrall Ridge is also the downhill finish of the Llanthony Show fell race and demands great concentration when going flat out. The run also follows a section of the Offa's Dyke path before returning into the valley, where the characterful bar in the Llanthony Priory Hotel makes a perfect ending to a delightful excursion through one of the prettiest places in South Wales. The priory ruins are also free to visit and well worth a look.

THE ROUTE

From Llanthony Priory the run gradually climbs via fields and a mountain path on to the Hatterrall Ridge. Here it follows the Offa's Dyke ridge path for three kilometres – with extensive views of north Herefordshire and beyond – before descending via a steep path back to the priory and enjoying views that will last long in the memory.

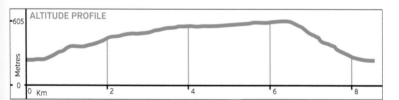

>> **LLANTHONY**

DISTANCE 8.3KM >> **ASCENT** 370M >> **MAX ALTITUDE** 605M >> **TYPICAL TIME** 1:15–1:45 HRS >> **TERRAIN** VARIED – FIELDS AND OPEN HILLSIDE WITH OBVIOUS, SOMETIMES ROCKY PATHS >> **NAVIGATION 2** – A HIGH-LEVEL ROUTE WHICH COULD BE TRICKY IN MIST BUT THERE ARE GOOD PATHS ALL THE WAY >> **START/FINISH** LLANTHONY PRIORY CAR PARK >> **GRID REF** SO 289278 >> **SATNAV** NP7 7NN >> **OS MAP** EXPLORER OL13 BRECON BEACONS NATIONAL PARK EASTERN AREA, OR LANDRANGER 161 THE BLACK MOUNTAINS >> **REFRESHMENTS** BAR AND CAFE AT LLANTHONY PRIORY.

DIRECTIONS » LLANTHONY

S From the car park pass back in front of the priory entrance and go through a five-barred gate; **turn right** and follow the track to another gate at the end of the wall – the way forward is signposted *Hatterrall Hill South*.

2 **Turn right** and follow the footpath across the bottom of the field – with the priory wall and ruins just on your right – to the field gate. Go through the gate and diagonally up and across the field to a metal gate in the middle of the boundary at the top of the field. A clear path leads up through woods – **bearing right** at a track fork – to emerge from the wood at a wooden gate signed *Hatterrall Hill*.

3 Go through the gate and climb the field on the obvious path (**ignoring** a stile after 50m on the right) to a gate in the intake fence at the top of the field. **Turn right** through the gate and follow a gently rising path for approximately 1.5km – sometimes muddy and rocky, but with wonderful views opening up to the right of the lower Llanthony valley. Towards the top, the path splits – take **the left option** to shortly emerge on to the main ridge path at an Offa's Dyke footpath stone marker.

4 **Turn left** to follow the Offa's Dyke path (gently uphill at first) for approx. 3.5km. The views to north Herefordshire with the Shropshire and Radnor Forest hills beyond open up to the right. You will pass a trig pillar and numerous piles of stones (**ignore** the occasional small paths left and right) until you eventually reach a large pile of stones with an accompanying Offa's Dyke tombstone marker (arrowed left to *Llanthony*).

5 **Turn left** and soon the path begins to descend with wonderful views down the valley and of the priory ruins. The descent can be sometimes steep and rocky (care needed). The path **veers left** at a small stream and zigzags past an unusual clump of trees to eventually reach a stile in the intake fence next to an information board.

6 Go over the stile and descend through the field on an obvious wide grassy path between the bracken (passing yellow-topped pole waymarkers) to a pair of stiles and through a small copse of trees to emerge into open parkland fields.

7 Follow the obvious path down across the fields through gates and stiles aiming for the right-hand end of the priory ruins to return to the first gate on the outward run.

TRACY PURNELL AND JON BARTON ON TWMPA.

09 ≫ CIRCUIT OF TWMPA   10km

INTRODUCTION

Twmpa, better known locally as Lord Hereford's Knob (honestly!), lies on the great north-west escarpment of the Black Mountains. While it's difficult to find the exact origins of its nickname, the peak has the obscure distinction of having an album track named after it, in the form of a satirical folk song by the band Half Man Half Biscuit (a song whose lyrics also include hills called Brokeback Mountain and Benny Hill!).

Quieter than its neighbour, Hay Bluff, Twmpa has a ridge, Darren Lwyd, that tapers away for about three kilometres from the summit. On this circuit you are likely to have the trails to yourself as you head away from Gospel Pass, down the Honddu valley, with superb views of Capel-y-ffin and Llanthony beyond and around the head of the ridge before climbing through a gorgeous, hidden and largely unknown valley to arrive on the edge of the escarpment below Twmpa. Here, after taking in the spectacular views, it's an extra ten brownie points if you can run all the way to the summit!

THE ROUTE

Initially it's a gentle amble down a quiet single-track road and then a boggy path across the hillside around the head of the Darren Lwyd ridge. This is followed by a delightful rocky path up a hidden valley to gain the main northern Rhos Dirion ridge of the Black Mountains (with spectacular and distant views) via a grassy but often boggy path. From here bag Lord Hereford's Knob itself before an easy descent back to the car.

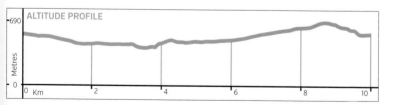

ALTITUDE PROFILE

≫ **CIRCUIT OF TWMPA**

DISTANCE 10KM ≫ *ASCENT* 280M ≫ *MAX ALTITUDE* 690M ≫ *TYPICAL TIME* 1:30–2:30 HRS ≫ *TERRAIN* VARIED – MINOR ROADS, OPEN HILLSIDE, GOOD PATHS (GRASS, MUD, BOGS AND ROCKS) ≫ *NAVIGATION* 3 – RHOS DIRION RIDGE IN HEAVY MIST WOULD BE TRICKY ≫ *START/FINISH* CAR PARK AT GOSPEL PASS BETWEEN HAY BLUFF AND TWMPA/LORD HEREFORD'S KNOB ON MINOR ROAD BETWEEN HAY-ON-WYE AND CAPEL-Y-FFIN/LLANTHONY ≫ *GRID REF* SO 236350 ≫ *SATNAV* NP7 7NP (NEAREST) ≫ *OS MAPS* EXPLORER OL13 BRECON BEACONS NATIONAL PARK EASTERN AREA, OR LANDRANGER 161 THE BLACK MOUNTAINS ≫ *REFRESHMENTS* WIDE CHOICE IN HAY-ON-WYE.

DIRECTIONS >> CIRCUIT OF TWMPA

S From the car park head the down the road (or, if you prefer, there is a faint hillside path which hugs the road just above it) for approx. 1.5km until you reach a cattle grid. To the right you may notice widespread boulder debris from ancient landslips.

2 Just before the road disappears over the cattle grid, **veer right** to follow a path skirting alongside or above the intake wall/fence on the left. (Note the large stone 'picnic table' – but perhaps it's a bit too early yet for jelly baby refuelling!) Follow this path, occasionally rocky and more occasionally muddy, for approx. 1.5km, passing the ruin of Waun-rydd and above a set of white buildings down below on the left: these are the former Capel-y-Ffin YHA buildings, now privately owned.

3 **Continue ahead**, passing a ruined walled field on the right and after roughly another 500m you will notice to the left of the path some prominent gravestone-like slabs sticking up. Shortly after these, the path splits, with the lower path hugging the intake fence and the higher right-hand path staying level and leading away from the fence. Take the **right-hand path**, which soon rejoins the intake wall/fence.

4 The path winds through some gorse bushes as it bends around to the north-west but soon opens up into a broad grassy track with a prominent tree line ahead – assuming that you can see anything in the mist. Head for this – keeping the intake fence/wall and hedges below to the left. The harder work begins here. Follow the obvious, grassy track ahead and when the path splits (with the right-hand path leading up to the trees), take the less steep **lower path** passing directly below the trees. When the intake wall bends sharp left your way lies diagonally down the grassy ride between the bracken to reach a minor road.

5 **Turn right** on to the road and follow it up (there are paths just off it to the right if you prefer). Pass through a gate and the yard of Blaen-bwch, then another gate to follow the obvious track ahead through two fields. In the second field, the track climbs and then runs along the valley side between two fences, before reaching a metal gate with a yellow footpath marker. »

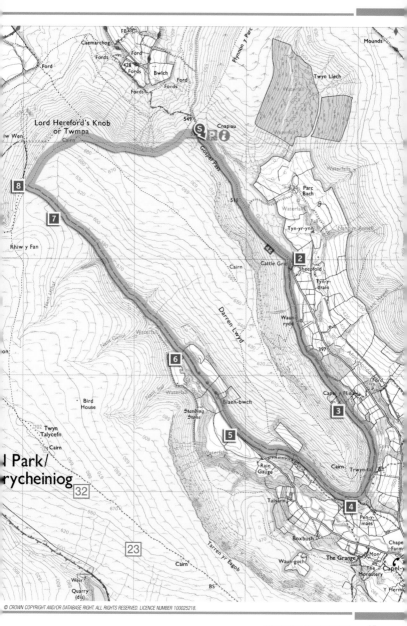

6   Go through this gate and carry on **straight ahead** along and then up the delightful (unnamed) valley with the tinkling stream below left, **ignoring** any paths left that drop to the water. Initially the path is a wide grassy ride, but it then narrows and becomes rocky (uphill only). Eventually the path crosses the (by now very small) stream. This is a good place to stop and take in the great views of the valley behind you.

7   After crossing the stream, follow the sometimes indistinct and often boggy grassy path due north-west until it reaches a junction with a wider (but also boggy) track. Ahead and to the left are superb views of the Brecon Beacons, Pen y Fan and the upper Wye Valley. If you get right to the escarpment edge you have definitely gone too far.

8   **Turn right** on to the path – initially level but soon becoming steep – uphill along the escarpment to gain the summit of Twmpa (full marks to those who run all the way up). The summit has a disappointing (and semi-permanent) cairn but no trig pillar – but it makes up for this as a wonderful viewpoint. From here it is a downhill dash along the obvious path. As you near the road, veer right on to a grassy track leading to the parking area at Gospel Pass.

DESCENDING TO GOSPEL PASS.

DESCENDING FROM THE SUGAR LOAF.

INTRODUCTION

The conical shape of Sugar Loaf mountain can be seen for miles, dominating the skyline of the surrounding countryside and providing a spectacular backdrop to the market town of Abergavenny. Its outline is reminiscent of a volcano, but the mountain is actually formed of the same red sandstone as the rest of the Black Mountains.

This run is a circular route up and around the mountain – one of the most popular peaks in South Wales, with easy access from Abergavenny. The gentle, rounded heather and bracken-clad shoulders of the mountain are crisscrossed with paths and provide an exhilarating place to run and take in the landscape's rugged wilderness and glorious 360-degree views across South Wales, the Brecon Beacons and into south-west England.

THE ROUTE

A short initial section along a minor road leads to a climb through beautiful native woodland followed by a broad grassy approach along the Deri ridge. A stiff climb to the Sugar Loaf summit takes in a spiralling circuit of the top of the 'loaf' with deep and distant all-round views. A thrilling headlong descent follows – and then a traverse across the face of the mountain before a final descent back to the start via fields, woodland and footpaths.

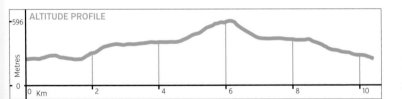

ALTITUDE PROFILE

Metres — 596 ... 0

Km   0   2   4   6   8   10

>> **SUGAR LOAF**

DISTANCE 10.2KM >> *ASCENT* 380M >> *MAX ALTITUDE* 596M >> *TYPICAL TIME* 1:30–2:30 HRS >> *TERRAIN* VARIOUS - FIELDS, MINOR ROAD, WOODS, OPEN HILLSIDE, WIDE VARIETY OF PATHS (MAINLY GRASSY WITH SOME ROCKY SECTIONS) SUGAR LOAF HAS MAINLY SANDY SOILS AND DRAINS RELATIVELY QUICKLY SO MERCIFULLY FEW BOGS, BUT THE ODD SMALL STREAM TO CROSS >> *NAVIGATION 2* – A POPULAR MOUNTAIN WITH A PROFUSION OF PATHS; COULD BE TRICKY IN MIST >> *START/FINISH* SMALL FREE CAR PARK (8-10 CARS) NEAR PORTH-Y-PARC (THIS AVOIDS A LONG SLOG UP ON ROADS FROM ABERGAVENNY) >> *GRID REF* SO 288166 >> *SATNAV* NP7 7HU >> *OS MAP* EXPLORER OL13 BRECON BEACONS NATIONAL PARK EASTERN AREA, OR LANDRANGER 161 BLACK MOUNTAINS >> *REFRESHMENTS* WIDE VARIETY IN ABERGAVENNY.

S   From the car park continue along the minor road to Parc Lodge, past a *No Entry* sign (access on foot only). Cross a cattle grid and pass a house on the left. Shortly after the track begins to rise, just after crossing a stream, **turn right** to follow an obvious woodland track (bypassing a metal barrier to deter vehicles). This woodland path is stony at first but gradually improves to become a real delight. Pass through a gate and where the path meets open fields coming in from the right pass through a further gate to emerge after a short rise at a cottage.

2   **Turn left** and go through a pedestrian gate to climb the obvious path through the woods. Continue **straight ahead** ignoring paths off left and right. At one major path junction **proceed ahead** (and uphill!). After skirting past a fallen tree the path emerges on to the open fell-side through the bracken – where glimpses of your Sugar Loaf destination can be seen to the left.

3   At a walled enclosure **continue ahead** – keeping the wall, then a fence, to the left – to eventually merge with the main broad grassy Deri ridge path. This is very runnable with only a couple of rising 'undulations' – and gives great views to the right of Ysgyryd Fawr (the Skirrid) and the Malverns beyond. **Ignore** any paths crossing either side and continue ahead on the main path as it climbs and levels out again. After passing just to the left of some woods the path then splits. Here **take the left-hand option** aiming for the head of the woods on the left.

4   Pass to the **right** of the field gate (**not** through it!) and continue along the path keeping the intake fence to the left. Just after a stile on the left (**ignore**), the path passes a low earth bank (with a couple of obvious trees atop) and just beyond take the path **turning right** uphill through the bracken. The bracken soon gives way to heather and (although always obvious) the path narrows in places to become single-track. At two prominent boulders the now-grassy path bends right and steepens to soon meet an obvious path crossing. ≫

5   **Turn right** (uphill – again!) and follow this occasionally rocky path up and around the summit of the mountain. (**Ignore** paths off to the left which take a more direct route to the summit.) This 'spiralling' path provides a relatively easy ascent to the summit and affords wonderful views to the main Black Mountains ridges ahead. As the path nears the summit ridge the elegant trig pillar can be spotted above and to the left – and must be touched.

6   Retrace your steps for approximately 30m from the trig pillar and then take the obvious descending path **south-west** which is steep and rocky at first but gradually levels out into a broad 'dual carriageway' grassy path (with an earth bank in the centre separating the two 'carriageways'). Try not to get too excited by the exhilarating headlong speed which you will no doubt have attained here – and look out carefully for the first path crossroads where there is a break in the centre earth bank.

7   **Turn left** to follow a grassy path contouring through the bracken (with Sugar Loaf's summit ridge above left) heading to pass just above the solitary tree on the horizon. Keep **straight ahead** and **ignore** paths left and right to eventually cross a small stream/gully to emerge just after at a further stream and path crossroads. Continue **straight ahead** to a stile and field gate.

8   Pass through the gate (or over the stile) and descend along a path across the field. This meets a copse of trees and after passing through three stiles/gates in quick succession continues downwards along a path/track to a (new, at the time of writing) stile and gate followed by another field path alongside a line of trees. The path turns into a field track and passes through two more field gates/stiles – with another beyond at the end of the final field. From here follow the obvious path (with a fence on the left and an overgrown hedge on the right) to emerge through the Porth-y-parc farmyard, from where the farm lane leads down to meet the 'main' road (with a splendid solitary tree beyond) where your car will hopefully await you on the left.

SUGAR LOAF AS VIEWED FROM TABLE MOUNTAIN (RUN 3).

ALTITUDE PROFILE

415

Metres

0   Km   2   4   6   8   10

A COMPETITOR IN THE 2018 MAGIC ROUNDABOUT FELL RACE » PHOTO: ALAN NICHOLLS

INTRODUCTION

The Begwns is a beautiful area of open access land, owned by the National Trust, just north of Hay-on-Wye. It lies slightly outside the national park, but we've included this run because of its spectacular 360-degree views of the Black Mountains, the Brecon Beacons, the Carmarthen Fans and far into the heart of Mid Wales. A visit to the Begwns is often described as 'all the views, none of the climb'.

This route is based on the 'Magic Roundabout', a challenging 10-kilometre race organised by Hay Hotfooters running club. At the highest point, the 'Roundabout' is a small wooded area surrounded by a circular stone wall, built to celebrate the new millennium. On the northern side of the Roundabout, there are also views of the tiny church of Llanddewi Fach hidden in the trees in the valley below – one of the very few churches in Wales that has no road access.

This run includes tough little ascents and descents, but is all runnable and can easily be shortened to 6.5 kilometres by only running the eastern section, to the Roundabout and back. In poor weather, navigation would be difficult due to the lack of landmarks. Save it for a fine day when you can enjoy the superb mountain vistas.

THE ROUTE

It's a three-kilometre undulating run on grassy trails before you climb to the Roundabout with its stunning views over the surrounding countryside. From here, you descend a wide, flat grass track for a fast, enjoyable 1.5 kilometres. You then turn up a narrow track bordered by gorse before descending to the lowest part of the course. From here, a wheel-rutted track leads you to a shallow ford, before turning uphill just before the halfway mark. Running around the side of the Roundabout hill, you head back down to cross the road. It's then uphill again followed by a short, steep downhill and then a fast last kilometre back to the start.

> ## ≫ THE BEGWNS

DISTANCE 11KM ≫ *ASCENT* 200M ≫ *MAX ALTITUDE* 415M ≫ *TYPICAL TIME* 1:15–2:00 HRS ≫ *TERRAIN* GOOD PATHS/TRACKS. BOGGY SECTIONS IN WET WEATHER (EASILY BYPASSED) ≫ *NAVIGATION* 4 – WOULD BE VERY DIFFICULT IN POOR VISIBILITY ≫ *START/FINISH* PARKING BEFORE SECOND CATTLE GRID ON CLYRO–PAINSCASTLE ROAD (THE FIRST IF COMING FROM PAINSCASTLE) ≫ *GRID REF* SO 182444 ≫ *SATNAV* HR3 5JH (NEAREST) ≫ *OS MAP* EXPLORER OL13 BRECON BEACONS NATIONAL PARK EASTERN AREA, OR LANDRANGER 148 PRESTEIGNE & HAY-ON-WYE ≫ *REFRESHMENTS* BASKERVILLE ARMS HOTEL, CLYRO; MANY OPTIONS IN HAY-ON-WYE.

S   From the National Trust plaque, take the steep track to the top of the hill then **continue ahead**, level at first and then descending gently towards a distant ruined farmhouse, until you reach a stone track with small cairn of rocks. Cross this track and then, almost immediately afterwards, cross a broad grassy track and after roughly 10m you will reach a junction with a third track. **Turn right** on to this track, which descends initially and levels out, eventually bringing you to a small stream. Cross the stream and take the **right-hand fork** heading to the hilltop, where there is a simple bench (which can be seen as a small dot on the horizon from the stream). From here you can see the Roundabout ahead. **Pass just to the right** of the bench.

2   **Continue ahead**, descending past the left side of a small pond and then to the left of a larger one at the foot of a steep bank with three trees on the ridge line.

3   Take the **left-hand path** to climb to the top of the bank. There are now views of a lake down to your left and the panoramic Black Mountains and Brecon Beacons beyond. Continue until you reach a single-track road.

4   Cross the road and **continue ahead** through the gorse and across a sometimes-boggy section before climbing the obvious broad grassy track to the Roundabout*.

*SHORTCUT
To shorten the run to 6.5km, retrace your steps from the Roundabout and trig pillar to the bottom of the hill at the road, and follow the directions from point 14 to return to your car.

5   From the trig pillar (set off a little to the left of the walled enclosure) **continue ahead** (roughly west) on a wide track past two isolated clumps of gorse. This is flat initially and then descends to cross a stream. Aim for the left corner of the middle pond ahead. Just before the pond take **a track left** which rises gently and **veers left** to reach a junction with a wide track.

6   **Turn right** to join this track, which descends across a broad grassy shoulder. **Continue ahead**, dropping and then veering right to cross a small stream just to the right of a small group of trees and passing two concrete platforms on your left. »

7   Go **straight ahead** rising gently and staying on the left edge of the gorse for 200m until meeting a prominent track emerging from the right through the gorse.

8   **Turn right** on to this track passing a solitary tree and climb gently to the base of the ridge, passing a pond to the right.

9   Just before the track starts climbing again, **turn left** on to a track running parallel to and below the ridge. This becomes more rutted and drops downhill between hawthorn bushes and trees until it meets a fence coming from the left. Passing the fence corner, continue downhill – **straight ahead** – **not** following the fence line – and pass to the left of a pond. A track joins from the right; **drop left** to a stone track.

10   **Turn right** and follow the track for 400m to where it bends left (just after another track joins it from the left). Here leave the stone track and take a rutted farm track **right and straight ahead**, climbing gently uphill.

11   The track climbs and crosses a stream before **swinging left** along the bottom of some crags. Continue to the hedgerow, where a path joins from the left at a ford.

12   Cross the ford and **continue ahead** next to the fence, passing a barn. After another 400m, the track bends around to the right to pass directly beneath the Roundabout before veering to the left at a small stream crossing.

13   Here take a path **on the right** between gorse bushes (initially boggy). This climbs over and around the side of the hill (aim to pass just above the lone tree). Just after crossing a small stream, **turn left** on to a track which gently descends down to the road (which you won't see until you reach it).

14   **Turn right** on the road and then **immediately left** back on to the earlier track at a wooden post. Retrace your steps to the top of the hill and then drop steeply, this time taking the **left-hand path** down the slope.

15 **Staying to the left** of the pond at the foot of the slope, cross the stream (often dry) and follow this track **straight ahead**, **ignoring** a fork left and any cross-paths encountered. This broad, grassy track descends gently at first and then levels out before gently rising through the bracken to reach a track junction (after roughly 400m). Here a wide track crosses diagonally in front while ahead the track forks into two paths. **Turn right** on to the wide track which descends and soon turns into a stoned farm track. **Take the first grassy path to the left** and continue to the bottom of the hill to meet the fence and hedge (at a small stream crossing). Pass **straight ahead**, parallel to the fence line on your left and back to the parking area.

JEN SCOTNEY AND JON BARTON ON THE DRAGON'S BACK.

INTRODUCTION

This is essentially the route of the Waun Fach fell race, to the highest summit in the Black Mountains, with stunning panoramic views. Travelling anticlockwise means an exciting and very runnable descent down Y Grib, a long, narrow spur, known locally as the Dragon's Back. The grand finale of the run is the finish at Castell Dinas, the impressive remains of an Iron Age hill fort with a commanding view of the Rhiangoll valley.

Notwithstanding that Waun Fach is the highest point in the Black Mountains, the summit is bleak, boggy and (frankly) disappointing. Whereas it once boasted a trig pillar, this has now disappeared and the top is marked (sometimes) by a ragged pile of stones. But don't let this put you off what is a superb fell running circuit in a quieter area of the national park.

THE ROUTE

From the car park, it's just over a kilometre of quiet tracks and country lanes before you turn on to a bridleway that climbs the open hillside up to a col. From here you take a path ascending a ridge for a couple of kilometres to bring you to the summit of Waun Fach. From the peak, an obvious path heads northward over peaty and in places very eroded ground, following a largely level route to a cairn. Here you turn left to follow a superb descent down the spur of Y Grib, the Dragon's Back, which rises and falls for almost three kilometres, before a short, steep climb on to the grassy ramparts of Castell Dinas and a drop through fields back to the start.

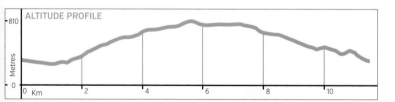

ALTITUDE PROFILE

Metres · 810 · 0

0 Km   2   4   6   8   10

» WAUN FACH & CASTELL DINAS

DISTANCE 11.5KM » **ASCENT** 620M » **MAX ALTITUDE** 810M » **TYPICAL TIME** 2:00–3:00 HRS » **TERRAIN** MOSTLY CLEAR BUT OFTEN BOGGY FOOTPATHS OVER HIGH MOUNTAINS AND OPEN MOORLAND, ONE SHORT ROAD SECTION » **NAVIGATION 3** - WOULD BE DIFFICULT IN POOR VISIBILITY » **START/FINISH** CAR PARK AT DRAGON'S BACK PUB AND BUNKHOUSE (PAY IN THE PUB OR CHARITY BOX), PENGENFFORDD, A479 **GRID REF** SO 173296 » **SATNAV** LD3 0EP » **OS MAP** EXPLORER OL13 BRECON BEACONS NATIONAL PARK EASTERN AREA, OR LANDRANGER 161 THE BLACK MOUNTAINS » **REFRESHMENTS** DRAGON'S BACK PUB, PENGENFFORDD (FRIDAY EVENINGS AND SATURDAYS ONLY, OTHERWISE TALGARTH HAS MANY OPTIONS).

LOOKING SOUTH TO PEN ALLT-MAWR.

Cwm y Nant

5

Y Grib

Pen y
Manllwyn

31

700

650

Twyn Mawr

600

775

550

450

Sheep
Dip

370

9

350

20

Rhiangoll

Waterfall

21

22

330

Ford

30

810

Waun Fach

4

800

Cairn

770

790

nyfed

690

620

Pen
Trumau

Cairn

570

600

Cairn

570

600

550

700

710

Cairn

Ffald Uchaf
(Sheepfold)

29

720

800

550

Rhiw Trumau

Cairn

3

500

Sheepfold

600

nant

28

Mynydd
Llysiau

663

Cairn

Sheepfold

Cwm-ffrwd

DIRECTIONS ≫ WAUN FACH & CASTELL DINAS

S   At the northern end of the car park, descend a set of steps (waymarked with a sign to *Castell Dinas*) and **turn right** on to a track. After 50m there is a stile on the left. **Ignore** this – it will be your return route at the end. **Continue along** the track, below and behind the pub, to a junction with three tracks; the left-hand track leads into a farmyard while the track straight ahead leads (through a metal gate) into farmland. Here **take the middle track** (which veers left) and after 400m you ford a stream just before meeting a metalled road (at a sharp bend). **Go left** along the road to pass farm buildings and a riding centre (where the road turns sharp right over a bridge). Continue on the road, uphill to where another road joins from the left.

2   Follow the road **around to the right** and then almost immediately **turn left** on to a bridleway. Initially this bridleway is stony and follows a streambed but gradually improves as it begins to climb the slopes of Rhiw Trumau, passing through several gates. **Stay on the main track** which eventually levels out and becomes less distinct before becoming a clear track climbing diagonally right up the hillside to reach the col and cairn. In clear weather, these are easily visible ahead of you on the skyline.

3   At the col, a grassy cart track (known locally 'MacNamara's Road') crosses from the right and drops into the valley ahead. **Ignore** this and **turn left**, taking the path uphill to climb the Pen Trumau outcrop. From here, the path (now boggy and rising gently) climbs for approximately 2km to bring you to the summit of Waun Fach. There are distant views; to the east, you may see the Shropshire Clee hills, while southward you may glimpse the Bristol Channel – with the Brecon Beacons and the Carmarthen Fans to the west, however the immediate vicinity is bleak, boggy moorland.

4   From the summit, **turn left** and take the obvious path northwards, descending a little and then skirting around the eastern ridge of the upper Rhiangoll valley. This path climbs slightly to Pen y Manllwyn (although this is not an obvious summit), and roughly 200m after this you reach a cairn.

5   At the cairn, **turn left** on to a faint, narrow path that drops down the hillside in a westerly direction on to the spur of Y Grib (initially a broad ridge but narrowing after the prominent cairn). As you run, stay on the top of the ridge, **avoiding** the paths to the left and right, which drop below the ridge itself. The ridge is predominantly downhill with short climbs to three separate summits. It is a lovely undulating descent, with views left, right and ahead to die for. Rocky outcrops and a cairn (sadly now less impressive than it used to be) are passed on the way down. Finally, at the bottom of the ridge, drop steeply to a gate and stile leading to the obvious Castell Dinas knoll.

6   Cross the stile and take the small, steep path up to the ruins of Castell Dinas. **Ignore** the more obvious path to the right as this bypasses the castle remains.

7   Run **straight ahead** through the castle remains to reach a fence (keep the various trees to the right and **veer left** to avoid the deep ditch). **Turn right** and follow the path alongside the fence downhill; after passing a small copse of fir trees, cross the fence at a stile and continue steeply downhill through two fields – keeping the fence on your right and **ignoring** the stiles in this fence. Cross the stream in the right-hand corner of the bottom field (to the right of the double-poled overhead electricity line) and over the stile on the opposite bank. Follow the hedge line round to the right to reach another stile which leads into the lane down which you ran (then all fresh, keen and clean) at the start. **Turn right** and after 50m you will see the steps on the **left** leading up to the car park.

JOHN PRICE SETTING OUT BY KEEPER'S POND.

13 >> THE BLORENGE

11.7km

INTRODUCTION

The area around the Blorenge is a UNESCO World Heritage Site and is one of the most significant early industrial landscapes in the world. The mountain is riddled with abandoned tunnels, forges and tram roads. With superb views of the surrounding area, this makes it a fascinating place to run.

The mountain is also host to two iconic fell races. The imposing northern slope of the Blorenge at Cwm Craf has brought many runners to despair as they scrambled up its steep face in the final miles of the Llanbedr to Blaenavon race. Perhaps more daunting is the downhill-only Blorenge race that, unsurprisingly, sees the occasional refusal at the top of the steepest slope!

Just beyond Cwm Craf is the Punchbowl – a spectacular bowl-shaped valley and pond. This was once the venue for illegal bare-knuckle fights, but is now a peaceful beauty spot and hidden gem on this lovely mountain circuit.

THE ROUTE

The run starts from the Pen-fford-goch pond (known locally as the Keeper's pond or the Forge pond – built to provide water for Garnddyrys Forge down the valley) and drops steeply before joining an old tram road to snake past old industrial works on the slopes of Cwm Llanwenarth. The track then circles the northern end of the Blorenge before passing the Punchbowl and through beech woodland before climbing on to the main escarpment ridge. From here it is over the top of the Blorenge (where there are fantastic views of Abergavenny, the Skirrid and the Sugar Loaf) and back to the car park on easy paths.

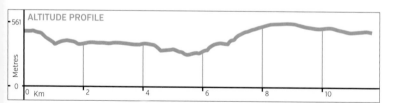

ALTITUDE PROFILE

>> THE BLORENGE

DISTANCE 11.7KM >> *ASCENT* 330M >> *MAX ALTITUDE* 561M >> *TYPICAL TIME* 2:00–2:30 HRS >> *TERRAIN* GOOD PATHS ON WIDE VARIETY OF TERRAIN – ROCKY, GRASSY, SOMETIMES BOGGY >> *NAVIGATION 2* – ROUTE FROM THE EDGE OF THE ESCARPMENT TO BLORENGE TRIG PILLAR COULD BE TRICKY IN MIST >> *START/FINISH* KEEPER'S POND CAR PARK OFF B4246 GOVILON TO BLAENAVON ROAD >> *GRID REF* SO 254107 >> *SATNAV* NP4 9SR >> *OS MAP* EXPLORER OL13 BRECON BEACONS NATIONAL PARK EASTERN AREA, OR LANDRANGER 161 THE BLACK MOUNTAINS. >> *REFRESHMENTS* GOOD CHOICE IN ABERGAVENNY AND BLAENAVON.

DIRECTIONS » THE BLORENGE

S From the information board at the car park take the path around the **left-hand side** of the pond. **Turn left** downhill to the road just after crossing a wooden bridge. Cross the road (**take care!**) and **turn left** and continue to a path signpost where you **turn right** on to the path. After **bearing right** the path reaches another signpost signed *Llanwenarth* after 200m – here **turn right** steeply downhill. After passing a rocky cliff-like section you reach a flat, grassy path at a signpost where you **turn right**, signposted *Garn Ddyrys*, and after crossing a footbridge the path (now level – for once!) **turns left** and follows the old tram road.

2 After passing an unusual rock feature (just off the path to the left) the path goes through some long-abandoned industrial works; **ignore** a path bearing right up to the road and proceed more or less **straight ahead** to pass under overhead electricity cables. The path continues up to meet the road. Run (**with care!**) down the road for approximately 200m and at the **second fingerpost** on the right-hand side of the road cross the road and take the obvious path (keeping the broken-down wall and fence on your right) signposted *Llanfoist 3.5km*. (This area is known as the 'Tumble' and the road is often used as a mountain finish in cycle races.)

3 This is now a level old tram road, and the way ahead is easy – just keep **straight on!** **Ignore** signs and paths pointing back to the Keeper's pond (right) and to Govilon (left) and keep heading for Llanfoist. The path is predominately grassy (but with some rocky sections) and wide through the bracken. There are wonderful views all along this section of the Sugar Loaf and the Skirrid – and latterly of Abergavenny below.

4 The path skirts past woodland around the head of Cwm Craf (with the imposing north face of the Blorenge above). The path descends (**ignore** an indistinct path to the right crossing the hillside) and then forks (with the left-hand fork descending to a stile and down to Llanfoist). **Ignore** the left fork but **keep ahead** initially above, and then meeting, the intake fence. After passing through a wooden gate the path drops before levelling out and then climbs gently to arrive at the Punchbowl pond. **Ignore** a path ascending to the right but **turn left** to follow the main path in front and to the left of the pond. »

5   The path climbs steeply away from the pond through an avenue of beech trees – and after curving right passes through a small pedestrian gate before levelling out and reaching a line of trees. Pass through two gates (one metal and the second wooden) to reach a minor road: **turn sharp right** at a wall junction (reassuringly signposted to the *Blorenge*).

6   Follow the steep grassy path uphill – sometimes staying close to the wall and sometimes veering away from it. After a short stretch through a depressed gully the path widens out into a rough track and gradually becomes less steep and follows the edge of the escarpment with wonderful wide-ranging views to the right.

7   When you reach the ugly square building turn your back on the views and pass by the building (uphill) via an often boggy and rocky path through the heather (directly away from the escarpment up on to the ridge). After the initial steep section the path levels out – heading somewhat erratically towards the obvious pile of summit rocks (which contains the Blorenge trig pillar); the path here can become very boggy in wet weather.

8   Pass by or over the trig pillar rocks and join an obvious stoned path leading slightly downhill towards a pair of communication masts (and the Foxhunter car park). Cross the car park and follow a path that leaves the car park access road just to the **right** of the fence enclosing the masts. This leads downhill (look out for occasional glimpses of the sea!) until you reach a wooden signpost. **Turn right** towards Keeper's pond, up through a narrow gully and **bear right** where the path splits (at a sunken path post). When the path emerges on to a lane **turn left** and just before the junction with the main road **turn right** to follow the path on the grass verge back to the car park.

THE VIEW OVER TO THE SKIRRID FROM THE CLIMB TO BLORENGE SUMMIT.

TRACY PURNELL AND HANNAH PHILLIPS ON THE APPROACH TO CORN DU.

14 » PEN Y FAN HORSESHOE   12.9km

INTRODUCTION

This classic horseshoe circuit links the peaks of Corn Du, Pen y Fan and Cribyn around a steep-sided glacial valley and is amongst the best ridge routes in the country, with spectacular views in all directions.

Pen y Fan is the highest mountain in southern Britain and the impressive sequence of steep escarpments around the peak forms the heart of the central Brecon Beacons range. Access to the summits is via the Graig Fan Ddu ridge and the return is on an ancient trail known as the 'Gap Road' (possibly Roman in origin), both of which provide fantastic running.

Despite some steep drops this route is not particularly exposed or dangerous, but it can be exceptionally exposed to the elements. Corn Du and Pen y Fan are popular peaks as they are easily accessed from car parks on the A470. Expect lots of walkers on that short section, in any weather.

THE ROUTE

A short section of minor road brings you to the end of the Lower Neuadd Reservoir from where it's a stiff climb to join the ridge. Here the gradient is mostly gentle over good paths as you continue to the summits of Corn Du and Pen y Fan. From here it's a steep descent then ascent to Cribyn (the latter can be circumvented) before dropping to Bwlch ar y Fan or 'The Gap'. From here it's a final few kilometres gently downhill on an ancient stony track back to the start.

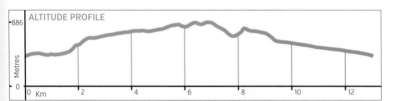

» PEN Y FAN HORSESHOE

DISTANCE 12.9KM » *ASCENT* 630M » *MAX ALTITUDE* 886M » *TYPICAL TIME* 2:30–4.00 HRS » *TERRAIN* EXPOSED HIGH MOUNTAINS WITH GOOD PATHS – ROCKY, SOMETIMES PAVED » *NAVIGATION* **3** – EASY IN CLEAR WEATHER AS WHOLE HORSESHOE VISIBLE AT ALL TIMES, BUT WOULD BE DIFFCULT IN POOR VISIBILITY » *START/FINISH* TAF FECHAN CAR PARK OFF MINOR ROAD FROM PONTSTICILL AND VAYNOR/MERTHYR. NOTE THIS IS A FURTHER 1KM UP THE VALLEY AFTER PONT CWMYFEDWEN CAR PARK » *GRID REF* SO 037170 » *SATNAV* CF48 2UT » *OS MAPS* EXPLORER OL12 BRECON BEACONS NATIONAL PARK WESTERN AREA, OR LANDRANGER 160 BRECON BEACONS » *REFRESHMENTS* GOOD CHOICE IN PONTSTICILL, MERTHYR TYDFIL (SOUTH) OR TALYBONT-ON-USK (NORTH-EAST).

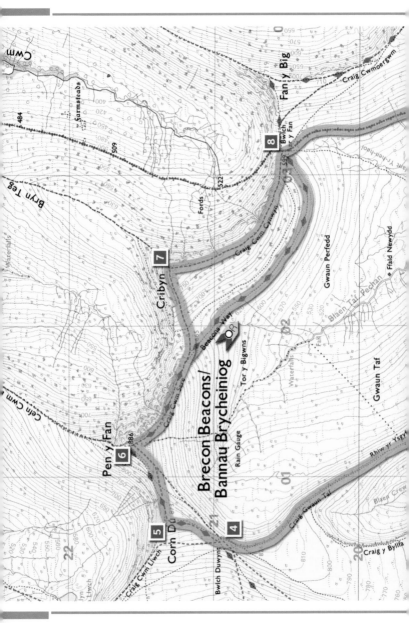

Brecon Beacons/
Bannau Brycheiniog

Tor Glas

Waterfalls

9

Ford

Tor Fechan

S

423

393

Rain Gauge

460

2

Filter House

Falls

FB

Fall

Standing Stone

Coetgae Du

450

Cairns

Weir

Upper Neuadd Reservoir

FB

Neuadd House

640

470

500

Twyn y Neuadd

595

590

Rain Gauge

3

BS

BS

642

600

Twyn Mwyalchod

570

580

590

560

Cairn

Graig Fan Ddu

730

720

710

700

690

680

Pile of Stones

Cairn

Beacons National Park/
...thol Bannau Brycheiniog

Waterfall

Gwaun Nant Ddu

630

620

610

600

590

...r Ddu

Waterfall

Waterfall

580

570

560

Waterfalls

Cwm Crew

Waterfall

19

18

17

S Take the path from the north end of car park to the road; **turn left**. At the path junction, take the **left fork**, signposted for *Neuadd* (making a note of the right fork which will be your return route). The track soon forks again. Here take the **left fork** and head for the obvious grove of trees approx. 1km away. Pass through a gate in front of the ruined waterworks building.

2 **Turning left**, descend on a path through trees to cross a bridge to the left of the weir and then ascend on to the earth dam. Cross the dam to a gate from where the path climbing to the Graig Fan Ddu ridge is obvious (but steep!)

3 On reaching the ridge, take the **path left** to make a short detour to pay respects at the 'military' trig pillar and then proceed **north-west** along the obvious ridge path – with gentle undulations and great views of Pen y Fan and Cribyn ahead.

4 After approximately 3km descend slightly to the col at Bwlch Duwynt – where, on a sunny day, you will probably encounter the hordes joining from the left along the Pont ar Daf 'motorway' path. **Continue ahead** to climb the shale outcrop to the summit of Corn Du and marvel at the views that open up to the north, taking in Cwm Llwch down to Brecon and far beyond.

5 After prising yourself away from the summit, **turn right** and descend briefly to the Craig Cwm Sere ridge (which links Corn Ddu to Pen y Fan, 500m away) and then climb to reach the crowds on Pen y Fan's summit.

6 Take your (no doubt reluctant) leave of the masses and with your back to the cairn, take the **left-hand path** that descends to the col below Cribyn – the way is obvious, down the 'staircase' (initially steep and rocky), first **south-east** and then **east**. Pass over the col* (with its small and lonely pool) and then climb up the steep but short pull to the summit of Cribyn, with its shapely peaked top.

NEAR-ZERO VISIBILITY AT THE HIGHEST POINT IN SOUTH WALES.

*OPTIONAL ROUTE

OR At the col at the base of Cribyn, there is an option to take a contouring path right which misses out Cribyn. This will bring you to the col of Bwlch ar y Fan where you rejoin the main route at point 8.

7 Descend (initially gentle but getting steeper) **south** then veering **south-east** to reach the col of Bwlch ar y Fan (The Gap).

8 **Turn right** to take the obvious stoned Roman road descending gently south. After approx. 2.5km the path forks.

9 Take the **left fork** down through a severely washed-out gully (the Romans would never have let this happen!) to cross a stream and climb to a gate and stile before continuing along the 'road' at the bottom edge of a fir plantation to reach the metalled road. **Turn left** and after 300m take the path **to the right** back to the car park.

ALTITUDE PROFILE

551

Metres

0

0 Km   2   4   6   8   10   12

JON DREVER ON THE STIFF ASCENT OF TOR Y FOEL ABOVE TALYBONT RESERVOIR.

15 ≫ TOR Y FOEL

13.2km

INTRODUCTION

Tor y Foel is wedged between the Black Mountains and central Beacons, but belongs to neither range. It's an impressive hill, yet not difficult to climb and provides far-reaching views – from the Brecon Beacons in the west to the Black Mountains.

Starting from the pretty village of Talybont-on-Usk, this run offers a variety of Beacons scenery, while also taking in much local history, including the Brinore Tramroad, an early 19th-century horse-drawn railway that provided a link between the canal at Talybont and Tredegar's ironworks and the Trefil limestone quarries. On the tramway, you climb above the scenic Talybont Reservoir, which provides water for the conurbations of South Wales and, after crossing Tor y Foel, return along a gorgeous, leafy stretch of the Monmouthshire and Brecon Canal, one of the national park's most popular attractions.

Tor y Foel is also the venue of a local fell race, but our route avoids its steeper paths and is chosen to give an enjoyable, flowing descent to the canal and then back to Talybont-on-Usk.

THE ROUTE

From Talybont-on-Usk, it's a steady climb on the old tramway, through forestry, rising above the shores of the reservoir. Eventually you turn off to cross a short stretch of moorland before starting the steep climb up the grassy slopes of Tor y Foel. From the summit, with superb views to the Beacons, Usk Valley and the distant cone of the Sugar Loaf, there is a delightful, long descent through a succession of pastures before a short section on tarmac road drops you down to the canal. Running along the leafy towpath and over the Ashford canal tunnel brings you back into Talybont-on-Usk, where you will be tempted to stop at a canal-side beer garden before completing the short distance back to the start.

≫ TOR Y FOEL

DISTANCE 13.2KM ≫ *ASCENT* 450M ≫ *MAX ALTITUDE* 551M ≫ *TYPICAL TIME* 2:30–3:30 HRS ≫ *TERRAIN* GOOD PATHS AND TRACKS THROUGH FORESTRY, FARMLAND AND OPEN HILLSIDE, SOME BOGGY SECTIONS, CANAL TOWPATH, SHORT SECTION ON ROAD. ≫ *NAVIGATION* 2 – FAIRLY OBVIOUS PATHS THROUGHOUT; PROFUSION OF PATHS IN TALYBONT FOREST WHERE IT'S EASY TO GO WRONG; TOR Y FOEL COULD BE TRICKY IN MIST ≫ *START/FINISH* CAR PARK, HENDERSON HALL, TALYBONT-ON-USK ≫ *GRID REF* SO 112228 ≫ *SATNAV* LD3 7YQ ≫ *OS MAP* EXPLORER OL13 BRECON BEACONS NATIONAL PARK EASTERN AREA, OR LANDRANGER 161 THE BLACK MOUNTAINS ≫ *TRANSPORT* BUSES STOP AT TALYBONT-ON-USK EITHER FROM BRECON OR ABERGAVENNY ≫ *REFRESHMENTS* CANALSIDE CAFE, STAR INN AND WHITE HART INN – ALL IN TALYBONT-ON-USK.

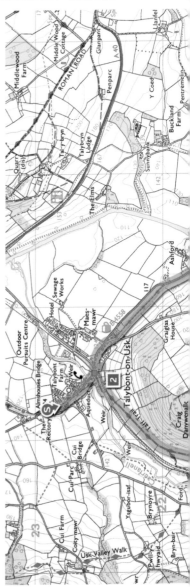

S   Out of the car park, **turn left** on to the main road and continue past the cafe, village store and Star Inn. Just before the White Hart Inn, **turn right** over the canal bridge and **immediately right** on to a lane. Continue **straight ahead** (**ignoring** a track to the left) and follow the tarmac lane that bends around to the left and over a road bridge. **Turn right** on to a rough track to join the Brinore Tramroad.

2   Continue for approximately 1.5km on the Brinore Tramroad until you reach a junction. The left fork is a path into woodland, signposted *Brinore Tramroad* and the right fork is a wide track, signposted *Taff Trail*.

3   Take the **left fork** and after a further 1km you will pass through a gate (with the dam wall at the end of reservoir down to your right). At the next junction take the **left fork**, staying on the tram road, following signs for a mountain bike route and **ignoring** paths to the right. This is a delightful section of trail on the edge of woodland, with lovely views over the reservoir. Continue until you reach a gravel road and join this to go **straight ahead**, ignoring a right-hand path into the woods (the mountain bike route). After roughly 250m and just before the second lay-by on the right, look out for a small footpath **left into the trees**.

4   **Turn left** on to this path, through a gate on to open hillside where Tor y Foel should now be visible ahead. Follow the track ahead, over boggy ground, until you reach the base of the mountain at a tarmac road.

5   Cross the road and **head left**, up Tor y Foel on an obvious path. It is a steep climb but eventually levels out to reach a small cairn where there are superb panoramic views. Ahead you can see the Black Mountains, while to the left is Waun Rydd, above the Talybont Forest and reservoir.

6   **Turn right** on to a path that takes you along the humpbacked ridge and then down the slopes of Tor y Foel on an obvious grassy path, eventually passing to the right of some woods. Ahead are wonderful views of Sugar Loaf as you drop through pastures, over a stile then through a gate, until you eventually reach a tarmac road at the bottom.

THE MONMOUTHSHIRE AND BRECON CANAL TOWPATH.

7   **Turn left** on to the road and, passing a house on the right, drop down the lane for roughly 500m. Just opposite a driveway on the right, look out for a bridleway sign on the left.

8   Take the bridleway **left**, across a sloping field, then pass through a gate on to a track past a house and parallel to a fence. Continue to a gate at the end, on the right, just after the wooden slate-roofed shed.

9   Go **right** through the gate and **immediately ahead**, through a second gate on to a canal bridge. Before the end of the bridge, **turn left** over a stone stile to join the towpath. Follow the canal towpath (navigation is easy here). After about 2km, the canal passes through the Ashford tunnel, while the path continues above (through fields, and briefly alongside the road) before rejoining the canal. After another 1km, the canal brings you into Talybont-on-Usk at the back of the White Hart Inn. **Turn right** to retrace your steps the short distance back to the start.

ALTITUDE PROFILE

802

Metres

0

0 Km   2   4   6   8   10   12   14

HEADING UP FAN FOEL WITH PICWS DU IN THE DISTANCE.

INTRODUCTION

The Black Mountain, or Mynydd Du, is the westernmost massif in the national park and is often described as its last surviving wilderness, with its peaty, upland plateau and sweeping, craggy escarpments towering above glistening lakes. This is a route to the best-known part of these hills, the unmistakeable escarpments of the Carmarthen Fans.

This run links a good access track with a spectacular ridge-top path to create an unforgettable tour of the highest summits of Mynydd Du. The circuit is full of interest – from the legend of the Lady of the Lake at Llyn y Fan Fach, to ancient archaeology and fascinating glacial features. The summit of Fan Foel is the site of an early Bronze Age (2000 BC) round barrow, now visible as a stone curb and central cist (a stone box made of slabs). When excavated in 2004, bone remains showed that this held an adult, a young child and an infant, as well as two pigs and possibly a dog.

There are options to shorten the route and miss out the second lake, Llyn y Fan Fawr, by taking earlier paths down from the ridge.

THE ROUTE

Initially you follow a waterworks access track for two kilometres leading up to Llyn y Fan Fach. At the lake, you take a good path climbing to join the western end of the ridge-top path. This continues east along the escarpment edge, above precipitous cliffs to Picws Du, the high point of Bannau Sir Gaer. From there, it's a steep drop to the col at Bwlch Blaen-Twrch before a stiff climb up to Fan Foel. After taking in the views and examining the round barrow, it's a short distance along the ridge to the trig pillar at Fan Brycheiniog, the highest point of the range, before dropping down to Bwlch Giedd where you take the rocky, steep path down to Llyn y Fan Fawr.

You follow the lakeshore before turning back towards the escarpment to join the undulating path along the base of the cliffs. This eventually brings you to the impressive glacial moraine at Pant y Bwlch, from where you follow a stream over moorland down to a weir and on to the original track back to the start.

>> **CARMARTHEN FANS & THE LAKES**

DISTANCE 14.3KM >> *ASCENT* 680M >> *MAX ALTITUDE* 802M >> *TYPICAL TIME* 2:30–4:00 HRS >> *TERRAIN* GOOD ACCESS TRACK THEN A MIX OF FAINT AND CLEAR PATHS OVER HIGH MOUNTAINS AND MOORLAND. PATHS MOSTLY PEATY WITH OCCASIONAL ROCKY SECTIONS, PARTICULARLY DESCENDING FROM RIDGE >> *NAVIGATION* 4 – WOULD BE CHALLENGING IN POOR WEATHER >> *START/FINISH* LARGE CAR PARK, HEAD OF THE SAWDDE VALLEY (KEEP GOING UP THE MINOR ROAD FROM LLANDDEUSANT AS FAR AS PRIVATE TRAFFIC IS ALLOWED) >> *GRID REF* SN 800238 >> *SATNAV* SA19 9UN >> *OS MAP* EXPLORER OL12 BRECON BEACONS NATIONAL PARK WESTERN AREA, OR LANDRANGER 160 BRECON BEACONS >> *REFRESHMENTS* NONE IN LLANDDEUSANT; CASTLE COACHING INN AT TRECASTLE; SELECTION OF PUBS AND CAFES IN LLANGADOG.

CLIMBING ABOVE LLYN Y FAN FACH.

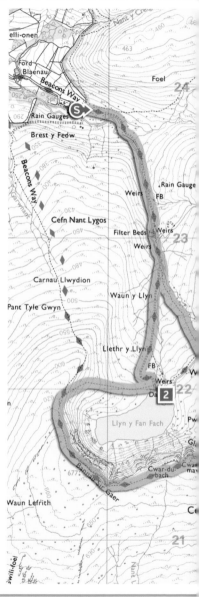

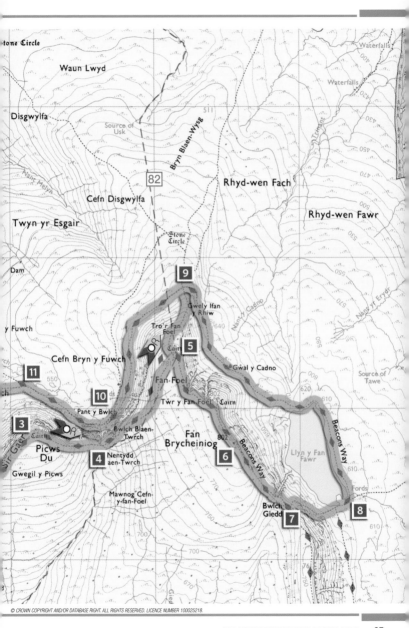

Stone Circle

Waun Lwyd

Waterfalls

Disgwylfa

Waterfalls

Source of Usk

Bryn Blaen-Wysg

511

82

Rhyd-wen Fach

Cefn Disgwylfa

Rhyd-wen Fawr

Twyn yr Esgair

Stone Circle

Dam

9

Gwely Ifan y Rhiw

y Fuwch

Tro'r Fan Foel

640

Nant y Cadno

Cefn Bryn y Fuwch

Cairn

5

11

550

Gwal y Cadno

Source of Tawe

Fan-Foel

10

609

620

610

Pant y Bwlch

Twr y Fan Foel

Cairn

3

Bwlch Blaen-Twrch

Sir Gaer

Cairn

Fan Brycheiniog

802

Beacons Way

Llyn y Fan Fawr

Beacons Way

Picws Du

4

Nentydd aen-Twrch

610

Gwegil y Picws

6

Fords

Mawnog Cefn-y-fan-Foel

Bwlch Giedd

700

7

8

610

670

700

76

750

S   Head up the track with Afon Sawdde down on your right. After 1km you reach a small trout farm which a path on the left bypasses before rejoining the track. After 100m look out for a weir, ford and path on the left. This will be your return route. **Continue ahead** on the main track. Straight ahead are the northern slopes of the Carmarthen Fans. After another 1km, you arrive at the glacial lake of Llyn y Fan Fach.

2   **Turn right** (west) up an obvious path climbing to the skyline. On reaching the ridge, the path curves southwards, continuing to climb gently with superb views of the lake below. This route is exposed to the left, snaking above precipitous cliffs, and **care should be taken here** (keep to the right if concerned). Pass a cairn on the right (the summit of Waun Lefrith) as the path curves around the ridge of Bannau Sir Gaer and up to the cairn at Picws Du. From here there are spectacular views north to the Usk Reservoir and into Mid Wales.

3   Continue along the ridge, which is level at first, but then drops steeply to the col at Bwlch Blaen-Twrch where the Afon Sychlwch flows down to the north.

OPTIONAL ROUTE

OR   The route can be shortened at Bwlch Blaen-Twrch by taking a (steep!) path from the col that drops to the base of the cliffs below the ridge. Rejoin the main route at point 10.

4   Cross the stream and take the stoned and gravel path (north-east) that climbs steeply, along the edge of the escarpment, to the summit of Fan Foel. Here, take a few moments to enjoy the views and inspect the Bronze Age burial cist – a circle of stone with a middle stone box burial casket.

OPTIONAL ROUTE

OR   The route can also be shortened here by turning **left** and descending on a path that goes north down the 'nose' of Fan Foel to meet the path contouring under the ridge. Rejoin the main route at point 9. ≫

5 From Fan Foel, follow the ridge to the trig pillar on Fan Brycheiniog. This is the highest point of the range at 802m and there are superb views down to a second glacial lake, Llyn y Fan Fawr, and to the Brecon Beacons to the east.

6 Just beyond the trig pillar is a circular stone shelter. Pass the shelter and **continue along** the ridge, dropping steeply on a rocky path to the col at Bwlch Giedd.

7 Just after the fence, **turn left** to take the rocky path (steep at first but gradually improving) that drops down to the shore of Llyn y Fan Fawr. From the lake there are superb views of Pen y Fan, Corn Ddu and the Black Mountains.

8 Follow the eastern shoreline, and at the end of the lake **turn left** and head along the northern shore back towards Fan Brycheiniog. The path climbs towards the base of the cliffs, and then away from the lake, before levelling out, undulating along the base of the escarpment. After roughly 1km, you meet the second optional route path dropping down the 'nose' of Fan Foel.

9 Continue on the path in a westerly direction before it turns southwards around the head of a valley, following the base of the escarpment. At one point the path narrows to cut along the cliff with steep ground above and below – **take care here!** Stay on this path to Pant y Bwlch, where you meet the first optional route path coming down from the ridge above, just after crossing a stream. In the valley to your right you can see a snaking linear mound, which is a glacial moraine.

10 Keep following the path along the base of the cliffs of Bannau Sir Gaer, towards Llyn y Fan Fach, to a point where the track divides.

11 When the track divides, take the **left-hand path** (west) and after roughly 400m you will reach a path junction. Here **turn right** to continue to a small bridge over a stone-lined channel, which diverts part of the Afon Sychlwch into Llyn y Fan Fach. Cross the bridge and **continue ahead** to eventually reach the ford at the weir above the trout farm. Cross the ford and rejoin the access track. From here, retrace your footsteps to the start.

ALTITUDE PROFILE

Metres

292

0

0 Km   2   4   6   8   10   12   14

THE STUNNING WATERFALL OF SGWD Y PANNWR » PHOTO: TRACY PURNELL

INTRODUCTION

On the southern edge of Fforest Fawr, where the sandstone that makes up much of the national park gives way to limestone, you will find the highest concentration of waterfalls in Wales. Known as Waterfall Country, here the rivers Hepste, Nedd Fechan, Mellte and Pyrddin drop down deep, wooded gorges over a series of falls, before joining the River Neath.

This classic route links all the area's most spectacular waterfalls in one exhilarating circuit. The highlight is passing behind Sgwd yr Eira, the Fall of Snow, on a rocky ledge between the thundering curtain of water and the cliff face. Don't worry: a pronounced overhang prevents you from getting too wet!

This run is an undulating circuit on a mix of good trails and paths that are slippery, rocky, rooty and exposed in places. Care must be taken and the run should not be rushed. You will find it well worth the time and effort.

THE ROUTE

From Cwm Porth you follow the Afon Mellte downstream, passing through woodland and meadows to a viewpoint overlooking Sgwd Clun-gwyn. From here, you follow a good path along the rim of the gorge (with the option of viewing two other falls) before dropping into the gorge and behind Sgwd yr Eira. It's a steep climb from the waterfall to join a path that takes you via moorland and woods down to Craig y Ddinas. Shortly after this you reach Pontneddfechan, with a chance for refreshments, before a lovely section on a good-quality path along the Nedd Fechan to Pont Melin-fach, passing a number of smaller falls on the way.

Between Pont Melin-fach and Pont Rhyd-y-cnau, the path through the gorge is narrow, undulating and rough and may take longer than you expect. From the river it's a steep climb before a delightful bridleway drops you gently back to the start.

>> THE WATERFALLS ROUNDABOUT

DISTANCE 14.7KM » *ASCENT* 360M » *MAX ALTITUDE* 292M » *TYPICAL TIME* 2:30–4:00 HRS » *TERRAIN* VARIED – GENERALLY GOOD TRAILS BUT WITH SOME VERY ROUGH, ROCKY, ROOTY, NARROW PATHS WHICH ARE TECHNICAL IN PLACES, OFTEN SLIPPERY AND MUDDY, WITH EXPOSED SECTIONS (SLIPPERY BEHIND WATERFALL) » *NAVIGATION* 2 – A PROFUSION OF WELL-MADE PATHS IN THE FIRST HALF AND IT WOULD BE EASY TO TAKE THE WRONG ONE » *START/FINISH* PAY AND DISPLAY CAR PARK, CWM PORTH » *GRID REF* SN 928124 » *SATNAV* CF44 9JF » *OS MAP* EXPLORER OL12 BRECON BEACONS NATIONAL PARK WESTERN AREA, OR LANDRANGER 160 BRECON BEACONS » *REFRESHMENTS* ANGEL INN AND OLD WHITE HORSE INN, PONTNEDDFECHAN; THE NEW INN, YSTRADFELLTE.

DIRECTIONS » THE WATERFALLS ROUNDABOUT

S Leave the car park and cross the road to join a path signed *Sgwd Clun-gwyn* and *Blue Pool*. This undulating riverside path runs between meadows and the Afon Mellte river to the right. It crosses several streams and is very rocky and rooty in places, especially where it drops close to the water (**care needed**). Eventually you reach a footbridge.

2 **Do not** cross the bridge, but **continue ahead** (initially rocky and steep), following a sign for *Sgwd Clun-gwn*. The path **bears left**, climbing away from the river (with signs for the *Four Falls Trail*). Carry on until you reach a signpost. (Here you can turn right and drop to a viewpoint that overlooks the Sgwd Clun-gwyn waterfall.)

3 From the signpost and junction, **continue ahead** on the path above the gorge (signed *Sgwd yr Eira*). The path crosses several streams with stepping stones and a footbridge. When passing an information board, **ignore** a path signed *Sgwd y Pannwr* on the right and continue until you reach a signpost (by a bench) signed to *Sgwd yr Eira*.

4 Descend to the river on a steep, stepped path and clamber across rocks and boulders towards the waterfall ahead (**care needed!**). Cross the wet stone ledge behind the waterfall and then climb out of the gorge on a rough stony path. This climbs first to a noticeboard (warning about rockfall!) before **turning right** up the hillside to reach a junction with an information board. **Turn right**, signed *Craig y Ddinas*.

5 This is now a delightful path winding through open moorland and woodland often with superb views of the Mellte valley. **Ignore** any tracks off to the left and right and stay on the main path (with occasional signs for *Craig y Ddinas*). The path drops to a gate and continues through woodland before eventually emerging at a junction with a track in front of a fence with the Afon Sychryd river below. **Turn right** to continue, level at first, before descending steeply to the car park at Craig y Ddinas. The path is slippery and worn – **care needed**.

6   From the car park entrance, **turn left** to cross a bridge and then **turn immediately right** on to a bridleway. About 100m before a house, **turn right** through a gate and across a narrow field to a footbridge over the river then up to a road. **Turn left** on to the road and continue straight ahead at the road junction to carry on to the Angel Inn in Pontneddfechan village.

7   Go behind the pub and through a gate to join a broad track signed to *Pont Melin-fach* and *Sgwd Gwladus*. This follows the Nedd Fechan upstream to eventually reach a footbridge, where the Pyrddin joins from the left. (To view the falls, **do not** cross the bridge, but **turn left**, signed *Viewpoint*, and follow the path upstream. After viewing the waterfalls, return to the bridge.)

8   Cross the bridge. **Turn right** and follow the sign for *Pont Melin-fach*, **ignoring** the sign right and bridge to the Cwm Gored silica mine. The path is narrower and rougher from here. Continue alongside the Nedd Fechan passing by a number of smaller waterfalls in the river. Eventually you will cross a footbridge near a viewpoint and then climb steeply through the woods before reaching the car park and picnic area at Pont Melin-fach.

9   Exit the car park and **turn right**, over a road bridge, then **turn left** over a stile on to a path signed to *Pont Rhyd-y-cnau*, **ignoring** the lower path left which drops down to the river. Follow the often narrow, undulating riverside path through the gorge (with the river to your left) until you reach Pont Rhyd-y-cnau, where a rough track bridges the river. **Turn right** up the track, which is signed *Cwm Porth Car Park*.

10 It's a steep climb through the woods, initially through a washed-out gully, then on a better path to a gate and then across open ground to another gate on to a minor road. **Turn right** and continue on the road to a T-junction. **Turn left** for a few metres, then **immediately right** through a gate on to a track signed *Porth yr Ogof*. Follow the track downhill until a blue bridleway arrow where you take a **fork left** on to a path. This runs between hedgerow and fields and passes through a number of gates, before eventually reaching the road opposite the entrance to Cwm Porth car park.

INTRODUCTION

Fan Brycheiniog (802m) is the highest peak in the Black Mountain (Mynydd Du) region of the national park. The views are spectacular and reveal the isolation of the range – often called the last wilderness in the Brecon Beacons – especially when compared with the central Beacons to the east. On a clear day, you may even see the Bristol Channel.

This route coincides largely with that of the Fan Brycheiniog fell race and follows a superb ridge to the summit then on to neighbouring Fan Foel where there are remains of an early Bronze Age round barrow. The return journey takes you past the remote mountain lake of Llyn y Fan Fawr, along an undulating glacial moraine and through a delightful valley.

The route is exposed, so this run is for good weather. The drops are steep only on one side, but very gentle on the other, so there's no need for a head for heights.

For those wanting a longer day of ridge running, this route is easily extended to Bannau Sir Gaer further along the escarpment. For those wanting a shorter run, there is an option to miss out Fan Foel. See also the neighbouring Carmarthen Fans route page 85.

THE ROUTE

There's a short river section followed by a stiff open hillside climb to join the long undulating Fan Hir ridge that takes you to the summit of Fan Brycheiniog with Fan Foel just beyond. From here there is a steepish descent off the end of the ridge. Good paths take you past the mountain lake, Llyn y Fan Fawr, to pick up a trail along an undulating glacial moraine followed by a long rocky path descent alongside the Nant Tawe Fechan stream that takes you back to the start.

≫ **FAN BRYCHEINIOG**

DISTANCE 14.8KM ≫ *ASCENT* 660M ≫ *MAX ALTITUDE* 802M ≫ *TYPICAL TIME* 2:30–4:00 HRS ≫ *TERRAIN* VARIED – RIVERSIDE AND OPEN HILLSIDE, WIDE VARIETY OF PATHS (GRASSY, ROCKY, STONE FLAGGED AND SOME BOGGY) ≫ *NAVIGATION* 4 – EASY IN CLEAR CONDITIONS BUT COULD BE VERY DIFFICULT IN POOR VISIBILITY ≫ *START/FINISH* OPPOSITE TAFARN Y GARREG INN, PARKING JUST OFF A4067 IN LAY-BYS NEAR GWYN ARMS, TAFARN Y GARREG INN AND CALLWEN CHURCH ≫ *GRID REF* SN 849171 ≫ *SATNAV* SA9 1GS ≫ *OS MAP* EXPLORER OL12 BRECON BEACONS NATIONAL PARK WESTERN AREA, LANDRANGER 160 BRECON BEACONS ≫ *TRANSPORT* BUSES STOP AT TAFARN Y GARREG, GLYNTAWE, FROM EITHER BRECON OR SWANSEA ≫ *REFRESHMENTS* PUBS IN GLYNTAWE; CAFES/TEAROOMS AT CRAIG-Y-NOS COUNTRY PARK AND DAN-YR-OGOF CAVES.

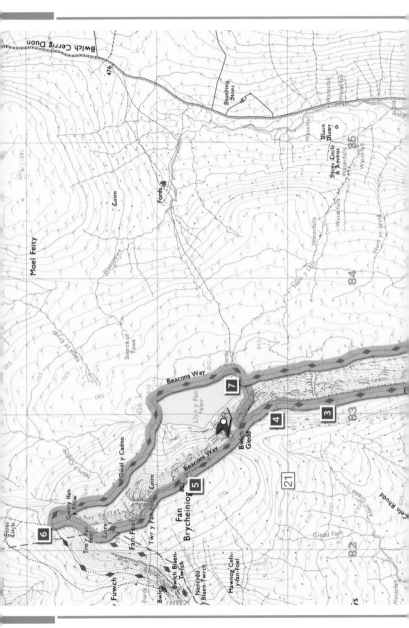

DIRECTIONS ≫ FAN BRYCHEINIOG

S Start on the footpath opposite Tafarn y Garreg inn, which leads over a footbridge **then right** along a riverbank **then left** at a metal gate on to a track between fences. Go through a further gate **then right** and over a stile. Make a note of a path to the right (signed *Beacons Way*) as this is your return route. Go **straight ahead** on to an obvious path which leads past the walls of a sheep handling pen to start the steep ascent of Allt Fach.

2 Follow the steeply ascending path (mainly grassy with rocky interludes) up and over Allt Fach (sometimes boggy) to reach the main Fan Hir ridge. Views open up of the upper Tawe valley to the east with the main Brecon Beacons beyond.

3 Nearing the top of the ridge, views of Llyn y Fan Fawr begin to emerge and on topping the ridge the main peak of Fan Brycheiniog appears ahead (beyond the col at Bwlch Giedd).

4 Descend to the col* and climb the stone-flagged path ahead to the shelter at Fan Brycheiniog (with its trig pillar just beyond).

*OPTIONAL ROUTE

OR The run can be shortened from the col by descending the steep rocky path **right** to the southern head of the lake and continuing from point 7.

5 From the trig pillar **continue ahead** to a cairn then follow the path as it **veers left** and **then right** passing a pond to the left and reaching an unusual stone circle (the remains of a Bronze Age round barrow). **Ignoring** the path to the left (which continues along the escarpment) **continue straight through** the stone circle to the end of the ridge (Tro'r Fan Foel) and descend on the obvious path, with the Usk Reservoir in sight 3km distant, to an obvious junction at the bottom.

6 **Turn right** to follow a path which swings around to follow the base of the ridge before dropping over moraine to emerge above the northern end of the lake, Llyn y Fan Fawr. The path descends to the lake and passes along its eastern side and crosses a stream before curving around the southern end of the lake to meet the optional route path from the col above.

DESCENDING FAN FOEL.

7   From this junction, **turn left** and head uphill away from lake towards the base of the Fan Hir ridge (on which you ran on the way out) on to a well-defined line of glacial moraine. Follow the undulating path along the moraine ridge for roughly 2km. At the end, just after passing a pond on the right, the path drops steeply into the valley floor. The path then crosses the stream to follow its left bank, before crossing it again later above a series of waterfalls (**care needed here**). It then descends sharply into the Nant Tawe Fechan valley. The path is muddy and rocky in places and descends through bracken-covered hillside to eventually meet the intake wall. Stay on the hillside side of fences/walls and follow the rough path to end back at the stile near the sheep handling pens at the start of run. Retrace your route down the track between fences, along the riverbank and back over the bridge to end on the main road opposite the Tafarn y Garreg inn.

ALTITUDE PROFILE

703

Metres

0

0 Km   2   4   6   8   10   12   14   16

JEN SCOTNEY ON THE OFFA'S DYKE PATH BELOW HAY BLUFF.

INTRODUCTION

Crib y Garth ridge (known locally as the Cat's Back), its summit, Black Hill, and its neighbour, the Olchon Valley, are all hidden gems in the Black Mountains. While situated just outside the national park, the location has featured in literature and film. Bruce Chatwin used the Black Hill as the setting for his novel *On the Black Hill*, while Owen Sheers' novel *Resistance* was based in the Olchon Valley. Both have been adapted for screen.

This superb circuit starts in Wales at Hay Bluff, crosses into England to reach the Black Hill and then follows the Cat's Back, one of Herefordshire's finest ridges, to plunge into the peaceful Olchon Valley before climbing up to the Offa's Dyke path for the return journey along a second ridge. The route offers two common features of the Black Mountains – wild, bleak ridges, and lush, isolated valleys. Running clockwise gives a superb descent down the airy, serrated ridge of the Cat's Back, with excellent views across Herefordshire, all the way to the Malverns.

THE ROUTE

We start with a gradual climb up the side of Hay Bluff. Then it's a few kilometres of easy, ridge-top running to Black Hill before the superb descent along the Cat's Back, dropping steeply at the end into the Black Hill picnic area. There's a short section of road before crossing the peaceful pastures and woodland of the Olchon Valley (shortcut possible), then a steep climb on open hillside to join the Offa's Dyke path on the next ridge. Once up high, it's again easy running on good paths (in places on stoned pavement) crossing the peaty upland, to reach the highest point of the Offa's Dyke trail at 703 metres. From there it's not far to the trig pillar at Hay Bluff, with its superb views of the Wye Valley and into Mid Wales, before dropping steeply down the escarpment's face to return to the start.

Note: you could also start this circuit from the free car park at the Black Hill picnic site (SO 288328, HR2 0NL) and follow the directions from point 4.

›› **HAY BLUFF & THE CAT'S BACK**

DISTANCE 17.2KM ›› *ASCENT* 680M ›› *MAX ALTITUDE* 703M ›› *TYPICAL TIME* 3:00–4:00 HRS ›› *TERRAIN* VARIED GOOD PATHS ON RIDGE (SOMETIMES PAVED), WOODS AND FIELDS. ROCKY IN PLACES DESCENDING CAT'S BACK. SHORT TARMAC SECTION ›› *NAVIGATION* 3 – HIGH-LEVEL ROUTE ON GOOD PATHS, BUT COULD BE TRICKY IN MIST. ATTENTION TO MAP AND DIRECTIONS NEEDED WHEN CROSSING OLCHON VALLEY (POINTS 4 TO 7) ›› *START/FINISH* OBVIOUS (FREE) LARGE, ROUGH PARKING AREA NEXT TO ROAD NEAR BASE OF HAY BLUFF ›› *GRID REF* SO 239373 ›› *SATNAV* HR3 5RJ ›› *OS MAP* EXPLORER OL13 BRECON BEACONS NATIONAL PARK EASTERN AREA, LANDRANGER 161 THE BLACK MOUNTAINS ›› *REFRESHMENTS* NEAREST IN HAY-ON-WYE; OR CROWN INN, LONGTOWN AND CORNEWALL ARMS, CLODOCK.

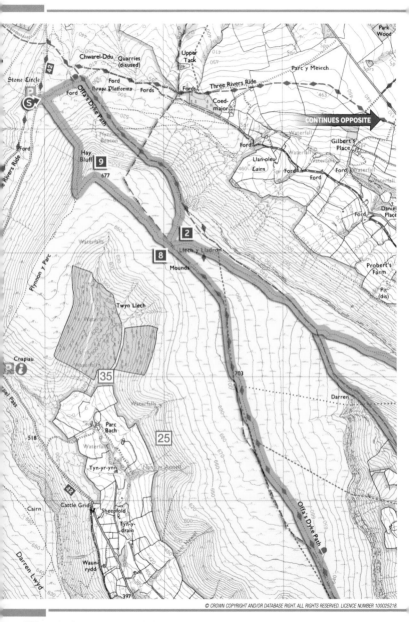

CONTINUES OPPOSITE

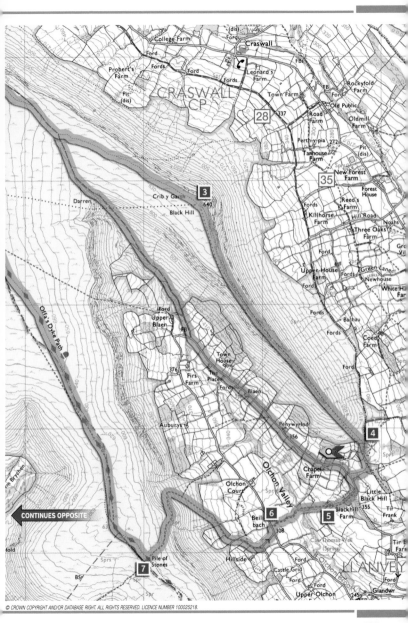

S From the car park, cross the road and follow the wide track that cuts **diagonally left** across the open heath in front of Hay Bluff. You will cross two streams and meet a track from the left – the main Offa's Dyke path. **Turn right** on to this to climb diagonally up the left-hand side of Hay Bluff. At the top, the path levels out and becomes paved. **Continue ahead** to a path junction at a stone signpost (Llech y Lladron). **Ignore** the arrow for the Offa's Dyke path that climbs a small hill straight ahead, but note that this path will be your return route.

2 At the stone signpost, **turn left** on to a wide track that skirts along the side of the hill. After roughly 1km, the track passes a large cairn on the right and soon after descends to a col (marked by a cairn) where the path forks. **Ignore** the right-hand path which descends into the valley (this would be your return route if you were to take the optional route described below). Instead, take the **left fork** and continue for a further 1km (**ignoring** a path left that descends from the ridge), to reach the trig pillar at Black Hill (there are excellent views of your return route along the ridge to the right).

3 From the trig pillar, continue south for 2km, descending along the Cat's Back ridge. The path is rocky in places and **care must be taken**. At the end, the path plunges steeply down a grassy hillside (very slippery in wet weather). At the bottom, continue over a stile and on to a tarmac road.

4 Follow the road downhill. This bends around to the right and meets a T-junction. Here **turn left***, then just after a metal gate on the right, **turn right** at a footpath sign to join a path through woodland following a stream downhill until it emerges in front of a house. Immediately on your right is a small gate into the grounds of the property.

*OPTIONAL ROUTE

OR There is an option to shorten the run slightly by turning right at the T-junction to follow a lane and then bridleway through the Olchon Valley, climbing steadily to bring you to the col referred to in point 2. From here, retrace your steps to the stone signpost (Llech y Lladron) at point 2 on the map and from there follow points 8 and 9.

To take this option, **turn right** at the T-junction and follow the (very quiet) road up the valley for 1.5km and, when the road bends to the left at the head of the valley, and just before crossing the Olchon brook, take the signed bridleway through a gate on the **right** which rises gently up the gorge to the col and on to point 2.

5   Go through the gate and pass in front of the house then drop to cross a stile. Cross a stream and follow the path on the edge of woodland then drop down and skirt the edge of some fields before crossing a footbridge. Follow the path to the left, crossing another stream then around to the right, passing a farmhouse on the right, before crossing a stile on to a lane.

6   **Turn left** and then after 30m **right** on to another lane, climbing steeply. It bends to the left and just after this, take the footpath **right**. This climbs through a meadow then **veers right** and contours along the edge of some trees. Cross a stile and a stream, then go through a kissing gate before dropping slightly to a wooden gate. Here, **ignore** the stile and path to the right and instead **continue ahead** on an indistinct path next to the fence on your right. Pass through another kissing gate and then cross a stream. From here, the path climbs steeply up the side of the ridge in a zigzag to the top. At the top, the track crossing in front of you is the Offa's Dyke path.

7   **Turn right** on to the Offa's Dyke path. Follow this for 3km, climbing gently to the highest point of the trail before descending to a small cairn and then dropping steeply down the hillside to return to the stone signpost at point 2. (Here you have the option to retrace your outward route, down the side of Hay Bluff, for a more gentle descent back to the start.)

8   **Ignore** the path to the right that you previously came up, and instead **continue ahead** along the paved path to the trig pillar at Hay Bluff.

9   From the trig pillar, take the **path left** (west) along the edge of the escarpment. After 400m, **turn sharp right** to take the path descending diagonally across the face of Hay Bluff. This initially requires a short scramble over rock shelves, before becoming a made-up gravel path. Where the gravel path ends **turn left** straight down a steep grassy descent, before the path levels out and returns you to the car park at the start.

THE VIEW TO CORN DU, PEN Y FAN AND CRIBYN FROM THE 'DIVING BOARD' ON FAN Y BIG » PHOTO: JOHN PRICE

20 >> FAN Y BIG HORSESHOE   17.5km

INTRODUCTION

Every July sees both hardened and novice fell runners tackling the Brecon Fans Race Weekend – two classic fell races with free beer, food and a village fete thrown in for good measure. This circuit follows the majority of the Fan y Big fell race route – the longer of the two races and badged as a perfect skyline run. Starting in Llanfrynach, the route encircles the deep Cwm Oergwm glacial valley via a lofty ridge. For those 'doing the double' there is also a 'short' race up and down Pen y Fan, the highest mountain in southern Britain, packing nearly 600 metres of ascent into six kilometres.

THE ROUTE

Initially it's across fields and minor roads from Llanfrynach before a steep pull up on to the broad grassy Cefn Cyff ridge (boggy in places) and a final short slog to the Fan y Big summit. From here a gently undulating path – varying between pitched stone, rocky, grassy, wide and narrow – circles the head of the valley with spectacular views on all sides before the long and gentle descent over the grassy Pen y Bryn tracks and then via minor roads back to Llanfrynach.

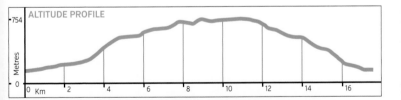

ALTITUDE PROFILE

>> FAN Y BIG HORSESHOE

DISTANCE 17.5KM >> *ASCENT* 700M >> *MAX ALTITUDE* 754M >> *TYPICAL TIME* 3:00-4:00 HRS >> *TERRAIN* VARIED - FIELDS, MINOR ROADS, OPEN HILLSIDE, GOOD PATHS [GRASS, PEAT, BOGS AND ROCKS] >> *NAVIGATION* 4 - HIGH-LEVEL ROUTE ON MOSTLY GOOD PATHS; COULD BE TRICKY IN MIST. ATTENTION TO MAP AND DIRECTIONS NEEDED FROM POINT 6 TO 7 AS THERE ARE SEVERAL PATHS DESCENDING BENEATH BRYN, BUT ALL LEAD TOWARDS LLANFRYNACH >> *START/FINISH* LLANFRYNACH VILLAGE CENTRE BY CHURCH AND PUBLIC TOILETS - STREET PARKING AVAILABLE >> *GRID REF* SO 074258 >> *SATNAV* LD3 7AZ >> *OS MAP* EXPLORER OL12 BRECON BEACONS NATIONAL PARK WESTERN AREA, LANDRANGER 160 BRECON BEACONS >> *TRANSPORT* BUSES STOP AT LLANFRYNACH EITHER FROM BRECON OR ABERGAVENNY >> *REFRESHMENTS* WHITE SWAN INN, LLANFRYNACH; WIDE CHOICE IN BRECON.

DIRECTIONS » FAN Y BIG HORSESHOE

S From the centre of Llanfrynach village (church and public toilets) go to the village hall and **turn left** on to a minor road. (This goes to Cantref but is not signposted as such.) After passing the last farm building on the right (400m), take a gated bridleway **on the left**. Keep the mill leat on your right and follow the path across the field into the trees. Follow an obvious path through three gates (with the river on your left).

2 After the third gate **turn right** up a slight rise and then **half left** to a gate/stile. Continue **straight ahead** up two gently rising fields (keeping a hedge, then a fence, on right). Midway up the second field (after passing a grove of oaks and a house) take a gate **on the right** and go **straight on** over two fields (with the fence and then a hedge on right) to emerge on to a metalled lane.

3 **Turn left** on to the lane (gently uphill) with views of Pen y Fan and Cribyn appearing on the right. Pass the entrance to Pentwyn Farm (campsite) on the left and **continue uphill** for roughly 1km, until the tarmac runs out. **Turn right** up a stony wooded lane (helpfully signed *Fan y Big*) to emerge on to open hillside.

4 The hard work begins here. Go up the steep grassy slope keeping the trees on your left and then up the centre of the broad ridge. The path (indistinct at times) follows a line of rushes and gradually gets less steep passing infrequent cairns as views ahead and to the right begin to open up. The Fan y Big peak comes into view (preceded by a broad heathery knoll) and the path (boggy in places) gently rises to the right of the knoll before a final pull to the summit of Fan y Big. Here the 'diving board' gives close-up photo opportunities with the classic 'breaking waves' view of Cribyn and Pen y Fan beyond to the north-west and the deep valley of Cwm Oergwm below. The onwards route is obvious on a clear day, and follows the escarpment path around the head of the cwm and descending via the opposite ridge.

5 From Fan y Big's summit, follow the escarpment path initially **south** (which while giving spectacular views to the left is never unduly exposed – vertigo sufferers keep to the right!), passing a ruined shelter and an old quarry and then continuing around the head of the valley. The path undulates gently and varies between boggy, bare earth, rocky, narrow and wide with long distance views to the Neuadd reservoirs and the South Wales valleys beyond to the south and the deep cwm and Mid Wales to the north. The path circles south, east and then north-east passing the Craig Cwareli 'corner' before reaching the broad grassy path junction at Rhiw Bwlch y Ddwyallt.

6 Here **continue ahead** on the main path, which becomes more grassy as it starts the descent towards the broad Pen y Bryn ridge and intermittently indistinct (sometimes no more than a sheep trod and at other times broadening into a wide grassy track). Keep **straight ahead** (north-east) as the path descends to the left of the ridge keeping the broad grassy lump of Bryn above and to the right as the wooded lower slopes of Cwm Oergwm leading down to Llanfrynach gradually come into view. Small streams and boggy patches are passed as the slope eases off. Pass to the right of a small group of thorn trees and then **aim to the right edge** of a line of oaks (with an intake wall coming into view below to the left). Pass an obvious dead tree to the left of the path and aim (again) **for the right edge** of (another) line of distinctive fir trees (with the village of Llanfrynach below to the left).

7 **Turn left** at the fence corner (near the middle of the line of fir trees) and descend to a gate/stile. Pass through and after 100m of steep descent take the **right-hand path** descending near a fence through trees to another gate and stile. **Turn right** (through the gate/stile) on to the track, past a large pile of stones to another gate and **turn left** down a metalled road. Follow the road down, over a bridge to a gate and road junction. **Turn right** (downhill) and at the next road junction **turn left** and after 200m pass over the river into Llanfrynach. Just after the red telephone box/library (!) **turn left** back to the start.

≫ APPENDIX

The following is a list of Tourist Information Centres, shops, cafes, pubs, websites and other contacts that might come in handy.

TOURIST INFORMATION CENTRES
Wales Tourism .... *www.visitwales.com*

**Brecon Beacons
National Park** .... *www.breconbeacons.org*

National Park Visitor Centre & Tea Rooms
Libanus, Brecon .... **T** 01874 623 366
.... **E** *visitor.centre@beacons-npa.gov.uk*

Hay-on-Wye
Chapel Cottage, Oxford Road
T 01497 820 144 .... **E** *post@hay-on-wye.co.uk*

Abergavenny
Tithe Barn, Monk Street .... **T** 01873 853 254
.... **E** *abergavennytic@breconbeacons.org*

Crickhowell
Beaufort Street .... **T** 01873 811 970

Talgarth
The Tower Shop, The Square
T 01874 712 226 ...... **E** *TIRC@talgarthcentre.org.uk*

Llandovery
Town Centre, Llandovery (Easter–Oct)
T 01550 720 693

Cwm Porth
Porth yr Ogof Caves .... **T** 01639 722 309

FOOD AND DRINK
CAFES
(See individual routes for recommendations.)

Cwtch, Abergavenny .... **T** 01873 855 466

Book-ish, Crickhowell .... **T** 01873 811 256

The Baker's Table, Talgarth .... **T** 01874 711 125

Shepherds, Hay-on-Wye .... **T** 01497 821 898

Casa Cafe, Brecon .... **T** 01874 622 229

The Old Printing Office,
Llandovery .... **T** 01550 720 690

Canalside Cafe,
Talybont Stores, Talybont .... **T** 01874 676 663

PUBS
(See individual routes for recommendations.)

The Bear Hotel, Crickhowell
T 01873 810 408 .... *www.bearhotel.co.uk*

The Grofield Inn, Abergavenny
T 01873 858 939 .... *www.grofield.com*

Brecon Tap, Brecon
T 01874 623 888 .... *www.breconinns.co.uk*

Blue Boar, Hay-on-Wye .... **T** 01497 820 884

Beer Revolution, Hay-on-Wye
T 07870 628 097 .... *www.beerrevolution.co.uk*

ACCOMMODATION
YOUTH HOSTELS
YHA Youth hostels can be found in the following places. For more information, please visit *www.yha.org.uk*

**YHA Llangattock Mountain
Bunkhouse** .... **T** 01873 812 307

YHA Brecon Beacons .... **T** 0345 371 9029

**YHA Brecon Beacons
Danywenallt** .... **T** 0345 371 9548

YHA Llanddeusant .... **T** 0345 371 9750

BUNKHOUSES, B&BS AND HOTELS
For specific information, contact a Tourist Information Centre in the area in which you intend to stay.

BUNKHOUSES
www.bunkhousesinwales.co.uk

Star Bunkhouse, Bwlch .... **T** 01874 730 080
.... *www.starbunkhouse.com*

White Hart Inn Bunkhouse,
Talybont .... **T** 01874 676 227
.... *www.whitehartinntalybont.co.uk*

Wern Watkin Bunkhouse, Llangattock
T 01873 812 307 .... *www.wernwatkin.co.uk*

CAMPING

Radnor's End Campsite,
Hay-on-Wye .... **T** 01497 820 780
.... *www.hay-on-wye.co.uk/radnorsend*

Bishops Meadow, Brecon
T 01874 610 000 .... *www.bishops-meadow.co.uk*

There are many, many more campsites in the
Brecon Beacons – try *www.coolcamping.com*
or *www.campsites.co.uk*

WEATHER
www.metoffice.gov.uk .... *www.mwis.org.uk*

RUNNING & OUTDOOR SHOPS
Likeys, Brecon
T 01874 622 900 .... *www.likeys.com*

Cotswold Outdoor, Brecon
T 01874 622 551 .... *www.cotswoldoutdoor.com*

Crickhowell Adventure
T 01873 810 020 ... *www.crickhowelladventure.co.uk*

OTHER PUBLICATIONS
North Wales Trail Running
Steve Franklin
Vertebrate Publishing .... *www.v-publishing.co.uk*

Lake District Trail Running
Helen Mort
Vertebrate Publishing .... *www.v-publishing.co.uk*

Peak District Trail Running
Nikalas Cook & Jon Barton
Vertebrate Publishing .... *www.v-publishing.co.uk*

Good Run Guide
Louise Piears & Andy Bickerstaff
Vertebrate Publishing .... *www.v-publishing.co.uk*

Day Walks in the Brecon Beacons
Harri Roberts
Vertebrate Publishing .... *www.v-publishing.co.uk*

Wales Mountain Biking
Tom Hutton
Vertebrate Publishing .... *www.v-publishing.co.uk*

ABOUT THE AUTHORS
Lily Dyu is a writer and a runner based near the
book town of Hay-on-Wye. Her childhood was spent
in Ireland and the north-west of England and her
love for the outdoors grew from studying geology
during a natural sciences degree. She started
running in her twenties and since then the sport
has taken her from pounding the pavements around
the University of Birmingham to running around
Manaslu, Nepal, the world's eighth-highest
mountain. Lily still enjoys the buzz of a big-city
marathon, but she is always happiest spending time
with friends, beneath open skies, and preferably
in lumpy places.

John Price is a solicitor and a (very moderate) fell
runner who hates running up hills – but loves
coming down them! After growing up on a
Herefordshire farm, he moved away in his early
career but now lives once again near Hay-on-Wye
and has spent countless days roaming over the hills
and mountains of Mid and South Wales – and
finishing near the back of the field in numerous
races. He has taken top podium place in the first
running of a local race (before anyone else knew
about it) and was also proud winner of a pineapple
at the 2017 Skirrid race (but sadly not for his running
prowess). A keen mountain-marathon competitor,
he has camped in boggy fields all around the country
in an unfeasibly small tent and always returns with
amusing stories of derring-do and misadventure.

ABOUT VERTEBRATE PUBLISHING
At Vertebrate Publishing we publish books to inspire
adventure. It's our rule that the only books we
publish are those that we'd want to read or use
ourselves. We endeavour to bring you beautiful
books that stand the test of time and that you'll be
proud to have on your bookshelf for years to come.

www.v-publishing.co.uk